✱ 6,9,102,10✱ 105

A
Life
of
Your Own

Harriet LaBarre

A Life of Your Own

A woman's guide to living alone...
with lots of friends...love...rewarding work...
and happiness

David McKay Company, Inc.
New York

A Life of Your Own

COPYRIGHT © 1972 BY Harriet La Barre

All rights reserved, including the right to reproduce this book, or parts thereof, in any form, except for the inclusion of brief quotations in a review.

MANUFACTURED IN THE UNITED STATES OF AMERICA

To M. S. N.

Contents

Introduction		ix
CHAPTER 1	Beautifully Alone? . . . Or Lonely?	1
CHAPTER 2	Who Are You, Really?	5
CHAPTER 3	With a Job . . . Without a Job	13
CHAPTER 4	The Money Side	29
CHAPTER 5	Where to Live: City? Country? Suburbs?	43
CHAPTER 6	Creating the Personal Background	51
CHAPTER 7	Entertaining	63
CHAPTER 8	Friends	95
CHAPTER 9	All Those Weekends	109
CHAPTER 10	How to Leave Home . . . Frequently	115
CHAPTER 11	Private and Personal	133
CHAPTER 12	Solitary Dieting . . . Drinking . . . Eating . . . Cooking	143
CHAPTER 13	Physical Security	161
CHAPTER 14	The Need for Love	171
CHAPTER 15	Affairs	187
CHAPTER 16	What's Around the Corner?	207

Introduction

This is not a man-trap book. It is a book for brand-new live-aloners and for women who are already living alone in towns and cities, houses and apartments, and who want to grow, want to like themselves more, have more friends, and really enjoy life.

It doesn't matter whether you're living alone temporarily or permanently—either way, you're entitled to the best things in life. Those best things can involve love, friends, money, aesthetics, growth, creativity, and a variety of other delightful pleasures. Whether you get them or not is up to you but it doesn't, for one thing, depend on your age: I have friends of all ages, twenty-five, forty-five, and sixty-five, who live alone successfully, enjoyably, happily. And it isn't a matter of luck. It never is.

Money? Money is not the key, either. A woman can live alone successfully whether she's living on a small salary or a fat annuity. Invariably it's up to her. . . . I know a woman who lives miserably and gloomily in an expensive apartment, and I know a twenty-six-year-old secretary who lives in a two-room walk-up and isn't any happier. On the other hand, I know plenty of girls and women, some with tiny incomes, others with thumpingly high incomes, most with jobs, some without, who lead thoroughly enjoyable live-alone lives.

Who's living alone in the 1970s? A random sampling ranges

from a thirty-two-year-old biologist who lives next door to me in a two-and-a-half-room apartment to four-times-married women like Bette Davis who says she has now "learned to live alone" and does so in a Connecticut country house, to no-times-married Doris Lilly who wrote *How to Marry a Millionaire,* yet who prefers a glamorous live-alone state. The sampling could include women of the stamp of Germaine Greer who was once married for some weeks. It includes women of the quality of writer Eudora Welty who was never married and Jane Fonda who was. It includes divorced women and separated women by the millions, and it includes relatively young widows like me . . . in my case, for the last seven years.

If we want to be statistical about it, *30 percent of the adult women in the United States are widowed, divorced, never married, or separated,* and a tremendous number of these women live alone, plenty of them without having much fun. Twenty-five percent of men, incidentally, are in the same situation, and they're welcome to whatever help they can glean from this book.

You may be living alone through *choice,* as a staggering number of people in the 1970s are. Newly independent-thinking girls particularly are trying it out in quantities, some with disastrous results and plenty of cause for melancholy, since the bed you make for yourself often turns out to be very lumpy, not to mention lonely. Census figures report that in the last eight years the number of people aged fourteen to thirty-five who live alone has soared by 84 percent. Since very few fourteen-year-olds and teenagers live alone (at least to my knowledge), that rather odd statistic means that an awful lot of people in their twenties and thirties are live-aloners.

More unmarried aunts, older widows, and older people in general are living alone these days, some because they have no choice, others because they are clever and independent and choose to cold-shoulder the old-style traditional pattern of living with their families, where too often in exchange for the fear of loneliness they're treated like excess family baggage or combination dog- or baby-sitter, vegetable peeler, and childlike incompetent. One independent elderly aunt of a friend of mine departed her family six years ago and is now living happily in an apartment not much bigger than a telephone booth; for extra money she rents herself *back* to her family as a sitter, and they get charged the same price she charges other families. Meanwhile she has the pleasure of doing as she pleases and the luxury of privacy when she wants it, and personal daily choices such as eating pizza (her favorite food) at 11:00 P.M. without anybody nagging her. The live-alone pleasures are myriad, if you know how to cultivate them, and she does.

Knowing how, of course, is the trick. It makes the difference between aching with loneliness or prizing your solitude. It makes the difference between choosing friends and lovers or being used by acquaintances and predators, between having a fine time with enjoyable activities and exercising your own tastes, or frenetically rushing around, sometimes (or often) into the wrong arms.

Fifty years ago, the idea of a woman getting any happiness or enjoyment out of living alone would have appeared wishful thinking, unrealistic—a fantasy. In fact, thirty years ago when an unmarried woman wrote a little book pointing out that it honestly could be done, people were startled. Now in the 1970s living alone can involve anything from an intelligent use of the Pill to 747-jet-travel vacations to furnishing an apartment with furniture that looks like knocked-down parts of a roller coaster. Or it doesn't have to involve any of these things; one of the pleasures of living alone is that the choices are all yours.

That doesn't mean that even the cleverest woman who learns to live alone successfully will be in a constant state of euphoria and enchantment, in love with her live-alone life *every minute of the time*. Living alone is no more enjoyable *all the time* than is the most ideal marriage. There are times when you enjoy it and others when you feel you'd happily give it all away. So no, I don't claim that solitary living is an ideal state. But if you're living on that particular shore, a little digging can turn up incalculable treasures.

You can, in fact, have a surprisingly wonderful time.

*You are
your own
Pygmalion*

CHAPTER 1

Beautifully Alone?... Or Lonely?

Living alone is an art to be learned. If you take the trouble, you can discover how to do it with great personal style and satisfaction.

Or you can have a rotten time.

A lot depends on how you view living alone:

If you consider it as equivalent to having gained possession of the Kohinoor diamond, you're in a much better position to enjoy it than the woman who views it as a disaster or as a temporary discomfort like the Asian flu. The "temporary-discomfort" viewpoint generally *guarantees* a rotten time: I know one well-off divorcée who lives in an apartment so bleak that the blinds are dusty, the walls are bare of pictures, the draperies a set of horrors left by the previous tenant. The apartment is empty of anything warm or beautiful or satisfying, there is nothing to feed the soul . . . and never much interesting in the refrigerator to feed the body. Yet this bright, smart woman in her early forties has been existing this way for six years now, on the vague premise that "It's only temporary," that any minute, *any minute,* some magic will happen to change her life: Out of her cocoon, she dreams, she'll emerge a butterfly; this is the fantasy she exists on. Meanwhile she has a drawer full of magazine clips of how her apartment will look when, sometime in the future, *it* happens. She runs the rest of her life on the same order: superficial friendships, skin-deep affairs alternating with desperate loneliness, nothing real, nothing *permanent.* She would be much better off, she would be able to *start,* if she acknowledged that living alone is a way of life, a life-style that is perfectly good, that can be *very* good.

Feeling lonely and sorry for yourself is also seductively easy —and self-sabotaging. I know an unhappy young divorcée who through sheer loneliness sleeps away her weekend, "sleeps herself stupid," as they used to say in New England. I know a successful fashion editor of thirty who, alone more than two hours of an evening, resorts first to a single highball, then a double, then tears.

Inevitably, we come back to choices: You must have a plan or you can live like one career woman I know who lives in dread of the empty weekend and can't wait to flee from her loneliness back to the office. You can be one of those women who wear their drabbest clothes at home (clothes that belonged down the incinerator or should have been sent to a thrift shop years ago) and who eat dismal stand-up meals in the kitchen out of cans. You can be one of those women and girls who wonder hopelessly where they can possibly go on vacation alone without being in an agony of embarrassment on plane, ship, train, at a resort—so they stay home. Quite a considerable number of others are simply at a loss as to what to do: *Here I am,* a live-alone acquaintance of mine confesses she thinks helplessly; and her plans stop there. She is one of the legion of people who gnaw despairingly on a dry sandwich on beautiful, sunny Saturday afternoons, unaware how to reach out for a fuller life.

For every woman I know who lives alone successfully I can point to a counterpart who makes shambles of the whole business. All this boredom, uncertainty, and plain loneliness is a great pity, considering that an enviable life-style is right there for the taking. The point is, you *do* have choices. True enough, living alone isn't marriage, but it can certainly be better than a lot of bad marriages, dreary marriages, boring marriages. Also it can be astronomically better than marrying someone, *anyone* out of sheer panic of loneliness or cultural brainwashing. Besides, living alone is how you're living at the moment, for whatever reasons, so why not enjoy it to the utmost?

The utmost is both a creative and sensuous affair that includes all kinds of pleasures like taking hour-long baths without family members banging on the bathroom door or finishing a murder mystery at 1:00 A.M. if you feel like it. When you live alone your apartment can be a total refuge when you want the luxury of solitude and reflection. At other times it can be the perfect place for entertaining your favorite people. Your vacation is your own personal choice, whether you want to spend it eating beaten biscuits and jam and riding horses on a dude ranch in New Jersey or getting tanned and drinking Sangría on a beach in Spain. In the country, if you're a garden lover you can garden until it's too dark to see and then go to bed with only a glass of milk for supper, if that's what pleases you. Incredibly simple pleasures can be incredibly satisfying. Here, for instance, is a glimpse of the famous French writer, Colette, when she was in her thirties, and settled down to live alone in a cheap three-room flat in Paris shortly after her divorce:

> *Never before in my life had I lived alone. . . . When I have told you that two other small rooms completed my domain, I will not have explained or described its charm. . . . At times elated by a new happiness, at times sunk in a boundless and reasonless feeling of security, I know that I wanted to live and die there. . . .*

> *When I think about the jug of cold water and the jug of hot water set beside the rim of the shallow zinc tub placed in front of an open fire of wood and coal, I tell myself that this comfort could have satisfied me for years. . . . I remember the spherical piece of English soap, black and smelling of tar and roses, and how the sunlight danced in the water. . . .*

But such solitary pleasures are only a skinny slice of the living-alone cake, once you get the hang of it, once you jettison old-fashioned notions that hamper you, once you get a new slant on *Who is there to love me?*

The point is to plan yourself a life that is positively, genuinely as full and happy as you can make it. And that depends considerably on your attitude toward yourself.

CHAPTER 2

Who Are You, Really?

Who are you, really? essentially comes down to *Whom do you want to be?* You are your own Pygmalion. The fact is that, when you live alone, you alone must create your life, making and molding it into what you want. No one's going to help you, no one will guide you, you have no married partner to lean on or blame anything on. When you make a wrong decision the penalties are all yours. If you get into legal or personal hot water, *you're* the one who has to fish yourself out.

Altogether, this is a scary but exhilarating situation—and full of possibilities, what with having all the freedom in the world to turn your life into an exotic plant or common garden-variety flower. Any live-aloner in her right mind will set out to make the most of it.

The more independent you are, therefore, the better. So if you have any lingering, sachet-scented notions that being independent isn't quite feminine, say goodbye to them. Independence—or you might call it self-sufficiency—not only makes you admirably your own woman, which a live-aloner has to be, but inclines other people to see you that way too. It is an ironical fact that the more a live-aloner creates an impression of self-sufficiency, the more people pursue her and the more invitations she has to all kinds of social activities. When you appear self-sufficient, people love you more, invite you more, lay more red carpets at your feet. There is no getting around the fact that people do need people, but it helps infinitely to create the impression that you can pick and choose.

Oppositely, if you act pathetically dependent, you become a social burden. When people feel they "have" to ask you along to the weekend beach cottage because they've asked a couple of your friends, irritation sets in—they resent feeling obliged to invite you. In line with this, it is wise to recognize that nobody owes you anything, and any attempt on your part to collect will get you nothing but a view of some cold shoulders and, eventually, lots of lonely evenings.

But how do you achieve all this self-sufficiency, this independence? One big step is to gain a "woman" image of yourself. Plenty of live-alone women I know still have an inner "girl" image of themselves—they see themselves as girls, whether they're aged twenty-one or fifty. Playing the part of a girl, with its implied innocence, vulnerability, and irresponsibility is all very well when you're still in your teens. And plenty of older married women can, after a fashion, get away with it by passing all problems along to a husband they regard as a husband-father-provider-protector. Admittedly, playing the part of a girl is terribly tempting, since we equate it with youth. But when you're an adult woman living alone and you continue to be a "girl," you're ducking the responsibilities a woman alone must have—responsibilities that involve sex and all other personal relations. This kind of evasion squashes flat the chances of a genuinely full, honest, live-alone life. The bald fact is that in this day and age, any woman over the age of twenty-one knows what she is doing and what life is about. Eve did, after all, take a bite of that apple. Once you admit this fact and accept the responsibility of being an adult woman, you take a major step toward self-sufficiency, toward becoming Somebody.

A Somebody has all the advantages. She meets people on an equal ground. She has the satisfaction of respecting her own actions. When she has a love affair, she accepts the fact that she knows what she is doing, and if it doesn't work out she doesn't blame other people or her girlish naïveté.

A Somebody also invariably knows *whom she's trying to please* . . . and the answer to that one is an unequivocal: Herself. It never pays to worry about what the neighbors will think if you're entertaining a man alone in your apartment until 3:00 A.M., any more than, if you're naturally pensive, you have to feel it incumbent on you to act like a Mexican jumping bean at a cocktail party for fear they might not ask you back. Pleasing yourself is far more conducive to self-respect, and it is anyway impossible to please everybody else. The attempt can only end in self-dislike and a loss of one's own personality—and that's about the worst disaster a live-aloner can have.

A live-aloner gains admirable stature if, for instance, when she is offered a ticket to a symphony she is able to say "Yes, thanks" if she really wants to go, and "No, thanks" if she doesn't, instead of acting humbly grateful and accepting out of gratitude for being asked at all. You're infinitely more attractive to people when you're a woman who knows what she does and doesn't want.

Personal worth is what I'm really talking about here. Valuing oneself. And when you value yourself you're well on the way to developing your own personal style. You're not only Somebody: You're a Somebody that other people are interested in knowing.

Some live-alones seem to come by a personal style naturally, through some inner grace, and they could probably maintain it if they were cast away on a desert island with nothing but a seashell to comb their hair with. But anybody can develop it. Paying attention to *ceremony* creates personal style, even making a ceremony of something as minor as a Saturday noontime lunch of a sandwich and an orange, perhaps putting it on a tray and making a windowside meal of it. Dignifying any kind of routine is its source, and there are all sorts of aesthetic and sensuous satisfactions in it. I remember a Kipling-type story about an Englishman who was stationed in a lonely jungle outpost in India, and who kept his sense of civilization by listening to a phonograph record of a woman's beautiful singing voice, a voice he honored by dining immaculately by candlelight while he listened . . . but when the record was accidentally broken, the Englishman gradually deteriorated into a slipshod, bleary-eyed drunk.

A personal style begins at home, and develops from treating yourself well, *always* treating yourself well; so naturally it provides any number of pleasures that can burnish even the grayest day with gilt. Personal style means the difference between going to bed in a dreary old nightgown just because you're alone, or investing in a beautiful, soft-as-a-dove silk gown on the theory that a nightgown lasts years and provides you with a feeling of luxury 365 nights a year. It means that you feel it is occasionally worth it to shake a few expensive drops of perfume on your pillowcase; it means turning your home into a haven of privacy and luxurious solitude that reflects your personality and eases your soul. An old bathrobe with a raveled cord belt doesn't suit *anybody's* style, of an evening spent reading a book. And it certainly doesn't ease the soul. It is infinitely more thoughtful of oneself to spend that particular evening showered and in a glow of well-being, wearing satin pajamas or harem pants or whatever suits your style. I know a woman whose personal style includes never rushing—though she is always on time; this doesn't particularly surprise me, since I've noticed that people who develop a personal style, a personal *worth*, become essentially self-contained individuals who generally do get where they're going without rushing.

In essence, you develop a personal poetry. And you carry it over into your relationship with other people. I can liken it to the effect the Gerald Murphys, those friends of F. Scott Fitzgerald in the 1920s had on people, as described by a contemporary critic as "an appreciation of art and music, a sureness of self and a delight in showing others how beautiful certain experiences, a sunset or a fugue, can be. I mean a kind of enthusiasm that is contagious, a kind of sensuality, a pleasure in the moment which denies distraction and anxiety, those worms that gnaw at the corners of our consciousness. When we are with such friends, we feel good about ourselves—and they have made us feel so."

Naturally, when you make people feel good about themselves, you create a . . . well, an *emotional climate* that draws people in. They react as though they were flowers blossoming under an extra quality of sunlight. They enjoy being with you. Some people expect, without really thinking about it, that some of your gold-dust will rub off on them. You have an enviable ability to make a party out of only apples, a jar of honey, a loaf of bread, and a couple of teabags? They'd like to learn how, too, maybe by osmosis, maybe by sticking close to you. *You* have spent some solitary evenings learning two or three French ballads? Maybe *they* can pick up the words to one of them. *You* have a way of viewing the day's problems with a sense of humor? Maybe they can, too.

Some people unconsciously develop a personal style by imitation, shaping themselves on the style of someone who has captured their imagination—a teacher, a friend, someone in history, even a character in a book . . . just as some fiction writers read a chapter of a writer whose style they admire before settling down at the typewriter. *If only I could be like her* is not a bad start toward becoming a Somebody.

One good rule, if you're going to become a Somebody, is not to brood over whatever boats you've missed. It is no use wasting time feeling regretful that you haven't been terribly clever about managing your life in the first place (or what are you doing here alone?). The boats missed are legion. "If only I'd divorced him earlier, when I was younger!" a forty-five-year-old divorcée laments to me. Another, who is thirty-five, tells me regretfully, "I should never have left my husband." *I should have . . . I shouldn't have . . . Why didn't I marry him? . . . If only. . . .* The one thing those boats have in common is that they're gone. You'll get a lot more out of life by turning your energies toward catching a few that could be satisfying. Being bitter about what

you've missed only makes you surly. And sighing and lamenting to other people only makes you a bore.

Or maybe you're among those live-aloners who thinks of herself as a Have-Not. That, too, is a great waste of time—not to mention that it promotes a needless but knife-twisting envy of married friends. Traditionally, since Victorian times, a woman alone was supposed to feel neglected and sorry for herself, a Have-Not. But since Have-Nots have taken to jet travel, skis, fighting for public office, or acting in underground movies, it is a laughable state of affairs to consider yourself a Have-Not. The live-aloner who feels that way is her own *saboteuse*. In the 1970s the word for a woman who lives alone and feels sorry for herself is "masochist"—there are, simply, too many pleasures and activities at hand to feel that way.

Sometimes a woman who has come to the live-alone state through divorce, widowhood, or separation unwittingly has a mountain of "we" habits she'll have to demolish before becoming genuinely herself. "'We' always liked musical comedies," a live-alone acquaintance I meet at a friend's home tells me wistfully. She is a widow of four years, pretty, but with tastes that one could hardly call her own. "Our favorite cocktail was always Manhattans," she says when you ask her what she'd like to drink. Politics? "We were Republicans," she says—and she votes the Republican ticket. "We liked waffles for breakfast." . . . "We always vacationed in California." "We liked musical comedies." This otherwise charming widow still vacations in California and buys tickets for musical comedies only. Presumably she eats waffles for breakfast. Her "we" comments about anything—a sunset, electric toothbrushes, the state of hippiedom, her opinion of modern art—reveal that she thinks of herself as half of a pair with the other half missing. Somehow, down some mistaken path in a happy marriage, she mislaid her personal identity. Now that she is alone she feels incomplete, a feeling that conveys itself the instant people are introduced to her; naturally she is not the most sought-after dinner companion or friend, so she spends most of her time alone, but not, unfortunately, in pursuits that are genuinely her own interests. *Who are you, really?* is a question she has not yet asked herself (though hopefully she will). It has not yet occurred to her that she can become a whole person, developing tastes and opinions of her own. She has yet to learn to savor the singular pleasure of saying *I*.

I is a very good word for live-aloners. I know any number of live-aloners who come from big, all-embracing families and who have to vanquish a "we" problem. "We like contemporary furniture," the visiting mother of a new-to-living-alone, thirty-year-old teacher from Minnesota told me didactically, while her daughter listened. "No," the daughter interrupted quickly, thereby triumphantly at last asserting her own identity, "*you* like contemporary —*I* like French provincial."

Asserting your own identity can have spectacular results . . . as witness the case of this thirty-two-year-old who turned herself into a successful live-aloner, a magnetic person as distinguished from a pallid family product. Jocelyn was a business woman from Michigan, an expert accountant in her early thirties and physically of Junoesque proportions. When I met her she had been in New York for six months and was still trying to shrink her personality into the dainty-girl image her late mother had always wishfully tried to compress her into: Jocelyn's hair was in incongruous ringlets, she wore ruffled blouses, and her laugh was an artificial, constricted little trill. Her three-and-a-half-room apartment was full of fragile furniture shipped from back home. Given what Jocelyn was, you could hardly expect her to be exactly awash with friends and social life. But Jocelyn had guts, and those guts, plus a lot of solitary thinking and reading on lonely evenings ("at least a thousand hours," she jokingly said later), helped her eventually to call in a secondhand-furniture dealer who carted off the family furniture. The other changes in Jocelyn's life happened slowly over a year, as she freed herself, and they must have involved many interior struggles. But they were certainly worth it. When last I went to one of Jocelyn's buffets in her now dramatically furnished, spacious apartment, she greeted me wearing a regal Egyptian gown, her hair in a magnificent mahogany-colored coil down her back. Jocelyn's laugh nowadays is a rich contralto that makes the wineglasses quiver, and she has plenty to laugh about. She has warm and interesting friends, including a well-known economist who is almost fiercely proprietary about her, and she is frankly, genuinely herself—oversized, not beautiful, but honestly herself.

Jocelyn's mother would never have recognized her little girl.

CHAPTER 3

With a Job...
Without a Job

Every live-aloner needs some sort of stiffening to her day: a spine, a *structure*. Otherwise, she risks deteriorating into a blob of jelly—bored, depressed, restless, lonely.

In fact, psychologists talk about "structure hunger" that, if it isn't satisfied, often leaves you feeling that every day is Blue Monday. Blue Monday people are easily recognizable: Here is Miss X, a divorcée living on alimony, and who, when the telephone rings in the afternoon, grasps it with a hysterical prayer of thanks, dresses, and rushes out to whatever last-minute invitation has been offered, not even stopping to think *Do I want to go?* but only hurrying to escape from boredom and emptiness into some activity, any activity. . . . Here is Y, whose father left her a small income and who is always tearing around on a merry-go-round of pointless engagements, but overcome by fear and panic whenever she momentarily finds herself alone. . . . Here is Z, a widow with a fine crop of imaginary ills, visiting doctors, sure she is the victim of some undiagnosed and dangerous ailment; when she leaves a doctor's office in mid-afternoon she stands indecisively on the street, not sure whether she wants to go to a movie (but doesn't want to go alone), or should she stop at the grocery (surely there is something she needs?), or perhaps she should have a chocolate soda (but it is 300 calories and she had one yesterday).

A job makes a big difference in morale, not to mention the money it provides, though it is perfectly possible to structure your day successfully without a job (I'll discuss how, later on).

But one kind of job can do a lot more for the live-aloner than another, socially and in other satisfactions. So if you already have a job, take another look at it and ask yourself what more it delivers besides a weekly paycheck.

Some jobs are lonely and unsociable, and exactly what a live-aloner does *not* need. After all, you're already spending lots of time alone, aren't you? But other jobs have plenty of friendly, human contact that's as warming as a fur coat on a winter day. A switch from a lonely, unsociable job can be worth the trouble. One girl I know, bright, young, friendly, came to New York five years ago from Des Moines and got a secretarial job in a one-person office, even though she'd been voted the most gregarious girl in the class. Two weeks of the job, and she began to bite her nails; by the third week she was back at the employment agency, and within a month was working as an editorial secretary on a women's magazine. Her life is now full of daily stimulation and plenty of people, male and female, several of whom have become good friends. In fact, around deadline time there's so much going on at the magazine that it's a relief to escape to the tranquility of her apartment, wash her hair, and fall into bed.

Of course, you may have reached the point where your paycheck for a lonely type of job is so sizable that it buys you trips to the Caribbean or Europe. Or it has other compensations, like conventions abroad or fancy fringe benefits. In that case, you may as well view it philosophically, while at the same time keeping an eye out for a switch to an equivalent salary job that offers more satisfying human contact, or the possibility of widening your social life. One woman I know made her switch right in the same organization. She started as a secretary-assistant in a sports clothes manufacturing firm. Over the years she had worked up to an executive job that paid well but kept her penned in a frosted-glass cubicle, working mostly on schedules between factory and office, and feeling like a trapped butterfly. In desperation she began poking her nose into the enviably exciting public relations department across the hall. She finally took a night course in public relations and got herself transferred across the hall where life was pure bedlam and teeming with people she found fascinating. She herself has become more alive, more interesting, and is now certainly no trapped butterfly.

When you live alone, you're also free to take advantage of exotic jobs. Travel jobs for instance. You don't have to join the Navy to see the world—you just go. There's nothing to stop the live-aloner from traveling anywhere in the world if the job includes it. When you work for a travel agency or tourist bureau (or in a dozen other travel jobs) and the office head offers you a chance to go to Africa or the South of France on an "orientation" trip (a trip to familiarize you with that foreign country, and a lovely idea it is), you simply lock your apartment door and get on a ship or plane.

In fact, you can even consider becoming a travel agency manager yourself, and get the pick of the trips to the interior of South American jungles, trips down the Colorado River on a raft, or airline inauguration trips to Yugoslavia or wherever. Of course, you work hard when you're at your desk in travel jobs, and you often work overtime, at the sacrifice of some social life. But fully 1,538 travel agencies in the United States are now either run by a woman or partly owned by a woman. And 700 of these agencies are controlled by a single woman owner.

One advantage in travel jobs is that travel fascinates most people, so a live-aloner generally becomes more interesting to people —and more *interested*. The mother of a friend of mine, a widow from North Carolina, had spent her first year of widowhood in a state of depression. One afternoon she passed her local travel agency and stopped in for a chat. Coincidentally, the agent was at the point of nervous collapse since the agency manager, who had been scheduled to act as tour guide to a group of people going to Tanzania had eloped the day before. On an inspiration, the owner suggested that the widow, who had taken three trips to Tanganyika with her husband, act as guide. That was the start of a travel job. The formerly depressed widow now takes a group abroad once a year, and the rest of her time she works at the agency and bones up on new (to her) countries. More than that, she attracts people as though some kind of foreign glamour has brushed off on her.

Offhand, I can think of at least two dozen sorts of travel jobs that can add spice, one way or another, to the life of a live-aloner who likes that sort of thing—jobs for steamship companies, resorts (from the Marienbad type to ski area), railways, travel agencies, travel clubs for single people or families, public relations jobs for airlines or hotels, jobs on travel trade publications, jobs in tourist bureaus, and so on. Some jobs take you abroad, some give you free trips, and in some you have to fight fiercely to get away from your desk. Parties and socializing are plentiful. During the years that I was travel editor on a national magazine (a job that demands writing ability too), I discovered that there are probably more parties given in the travel industry—hundreds a year—to introduce people to everything from a new cruise ship to a new hotel to a "new" island, than there are political parties given in Washington, D.C., at embassies and consulates. If you like meeting people from foreign countries, you'll meet them in the travel world.

But suppose instead of wanting to switch from one job to another you don't have a job in the first place. And you have no particular training. Maybe you were a biology major in college but never worked at it. Maybe you were a pretty good secretary once, but you haven't touched a typewriter in years, so what good is that now? Here you are, wanting a job, maybe needing an income or maybe simply ready to disintegrate with boredom or loneliness. As Freud put it, work has a "greater effect than any other technique of living in the direction of binding the individual more closely to reality. . . ." That means getting more happiness by give-and-take, friendship, and so on. So you want a job.

If you've spent years depending on a husband, you're inclined to rate your abilities so low that you're discouraged to begin with. You might feel there's nothing you qualify for, even if you did teach high school mathematics in 1952 . . . except perhaps (hopefully) a Christmas saleswoman job in a department store. Or you may wonder if you can learn typing . . . or does your age stand in your way? *Brushing up* are words that loom large in the mind of a woman who is thinking of trying to get back in the job market. *Maybe I can brush up on my shorthand . . . Maybe I can brush up on stenography . . . Maybe I can brush up. . . .* A dozen bottom-of-the-barrel jobs occur to her.

But this is actually the perfect time for a live-aloner to think, "What have I always wanted to do?" "What would I *like* to do?" And not, "I might qualify as a stenographer."

"What would I *like* to do?" is an exhilarating thought, thick with possibilities. Why not aim for work that you'd enjoy, work that's a pleasurable activity? There are a dozen jobs that will suit your taste, your personality, a lot better than a dozen others, aren't there? There are jobs that will fire up your ambition, give you a goal, make it impossible to be bored, evenings alone or not. You may get irritated and frustrated and angry and exasperated, and maybe you'll feel overworked, but you won't be *bored*. The job will give you too much personal satisfaction for that.

Consider what really interests you. I know one woman in her late forties who lives in a farming area in Connecticut where she grew up. When her marriage fell apart five years ago and she refused alimony, she needed a job. She spent weeks job-hunting and finally ended with a choice of moving to Bridgeport and becoming a telephone operator, or going to work as a file clerk with a Hartford insurance company. But after some pondering she rejected both jobs. Instead, she borrowed some money on her small amount of life insurance, and borrowed some more money from her brother, as living expenses, and began preparing herself to pass the Connecticut state real estate board examinations. It took her some months of thrifty living, during which she learned that spaghetti and tomato sauce can be filling and a pound of chopped beef can be stretched almost as far as to Boston. But she also learned all about terrain and first and second mortgages and guarantees and surveys, and all about buying and selling houses and acreage. She now has a fully-paid-for five-passenger car in which she takes prospective clients around the countryside. She meets lots of people and gets lots of fresh air. In winter the car gets stuck in snow and in the spring it gets stuck in mud, and once she got frostbite, and she fairly often trips over barbed wire and occasionally she sinks knee-deep into swamps. Anybody in his right mind might hate it. But she loves it. As she says, "It's just what I've always wanted."

Maybe you'll have to go back to school to get a particular job that intrigues you. Well, why not?—you have all the evenings in the world to take courses. No one's going to complain if instead of cleaning the closets or doing the laundry you're out taking a course in accounting or French or bookkeeping. If you decide you're a frustrated Florence Nightingale and want to become a practical nurse, go ahead. One divorcée I know took a photography course and is now an assistant to a New York photographer. Most of her job so far consists of booking models, ordering sandwiches and containers of coffee, and rolling studio lights into position. But it is a toehold in a world that fascinates her. She now keeps her clothes in the hall closet of her two-and-a-half room apartment because her bedroom closet is a darkroom where she experimentally develops the photographs she takes herself. Occasionally she goes on Saturday photography trips with a man she met in photography class. There is no one to look after her and make sure she gets enough sleep (she says she doesn't have time to sleep) or to make sure she eats balanced meals (she eats whenever she gets a chance, which at least keeps her slender). But neither is there anyone to object to her bedroom-closet darkroom and the smell of chemicals in the apartment. She is having a wonderful time.

If you'd like to develop a specialty or have some talent but you think: *It's too late* or *I'm too old,* that's nonsense. Plenty of people bloom late (you may be one) because they didn't get a chance to bloom earlier—after all, Paderewski didn't start to become a concert pianist until he was in his fifties. Some successful women writers of children's books, like Laura Ingalls Wilder who wrote *Little House in the Big Woods,* and so on, began writing in their sixties. The Roman statesman Cato started to learn Greek when he was in his eighties, George Eliot started writing in her forties, and Grandma Moses picked up her first paintbrush when she was seventy-eight. In 1971 the world-famous sculptor Jacques Lipschitz, who just turned eighty, had to move to Italy because he has begun to work on such monumental-sized bronzes that American foundries simply aren't equipped to cast them. Lipschitz says he considers himself lucky to be starting on the largest commissions of his life at his present age because, he says, before this, "I wasn't ready for it." How he feels about his work isn't a bad thing to keep in mind either: ". . . if my work is good, if it's bad, I don't know—and I don't care! I don't *think* about it. I just love doing it. It's such a joy, every minute."

Enjoyment is the thing. If you're going to have to work, have a good time at it, whatever it is. Use your time alone, to grow. I know one live-alone divorcée who in her forties entered Cornell with only an indifferent high school record, a sum of borrowed money, and a stubborn determination. After an admittedly costly, hard-working time she emerged a full-fledged psychologist. It took her years, and she is still paying back the money she borrowed. But she is rapidly earning enough money to pay simultaneously for a good apartment and good-looking clothes. She is also adding to a small collection of paintings on her living-room walls, and she has dozens of stimulating friends. Four years ago, she would rather have been almost anybody else she knew. Now she says she can't think of anyone she'd rather be than herself. If you're in your thirties, forties, or older and can get up enough nerve and enough money to become a professional anything-at-all, you'll get a lot more than a paycheck only.

If you're attracted to a business career—banking, investment firms, manufacturing corporations—you'll need true grit, extra courage, *guts*. Women weren't even admitted to the Harvard Business School, for instance, until ten years ago, and they're not lovingly welcomed by big business even now. If you want to develop your natural, creative business abilities, you'll have to fight the prevalent and dreary old-fashioned nonsense that women who try to succeed in business are only out to castrate men. If you allow yourself to be intimidated by words like "castration" and "penis envy," you won't get very far. The fact is, the truth is, that if you're a healthy-minded woman, you want to succeed in business because you want to exercise your real abilities in that direction . . . but if you are a certain kind of neurotic woman you maybe do have something else up your sleeve. There are women and women, just as there are men and men. The *reason* a woman wants to succeed in business is what determines whether or not she's healthy or neurotic about it. And that, of course, is true of both sexes in anything you can think of, whether in making love or trading in coffee beans.

Of course you may not feel like blooming late or blooming at all. But you will generally have to know at least some skill if you're going to have a halfway decent chance at a worthwhile salary and an enjoyable place to work, with people you'd like to know. Being a good typist is a great asset. Typing is the best door-opener to interesting jobs, as any reputable employment agency will tell you. Typing is an important skill, when you want to get back into the job market, or even if you want to switch from a lonesome office to a lively one. One good thing for the live-aloner is that typing is the entrée into the active, hectic world of advertising, broadcasting, publishing, and a dozen other exciting fields. Typing can be a foot in the door to dozens of careers, even some you may not have thought you wanted. But once you're in an exciting office, it can act on you like the smell of grease paint to actors in the theater. I'm thinking of one widow who went back to work as a typist after a twenty-five-year marriage. She had no thought except to get away from her empty apartment. But the office was an advertising agency, the excitement got to her, and within eight months she had picked up sufficient extra skills to get an advancement that gave her more money (which she didn't need), more confidence (which she badly needed), and enough renewed interest in life to make her interesting to the new people she meets. She is now in the process of learning to write advertising copy and often doesn't get home until ten o'clock at night. She complains that she has no time to buy any clothes, though ironically the ad agency has several clothes accounts. But the men she meets seem to think she looks very very good in the clothes she has.

If you're lucky enough to be financially secure but want a job for the pleasures of human contact, of *doing something,* of getting involved and having more friends, don't be modest and shy about money. Anyone with a deprecating, I-don't-really-need-the-money-anyway attitude ends up with the dullest of jobs. It is better to be greedy. It is better to learn where the money is *whether you need it or not,* for the simple reason that the jobs that pay more money are more demanding, more stimulating, and the people you meet are more interesting. The idea, after all, is not simply to meet people in quantities (you can go to a political rally or a rock concert and find plenty of warm bodies) but to meet people who are vital and alive, people who are possible friends with whom you can go to the theater, go to dinner, invite to parties (and be invited)—in other words, people with whom you'd like to establish genuine friendships.

Besides, there is enormous satisfaction in demanding and getting the money you're worth. A little ego-satisfaction never hurt anyone. It warms the heart. And as you climb the business ladder you get more monetary recognition and get to like yourself better; besides, other people admire and respect you more and want to know you.

There's one exception to this rule of aiming for money whether you need it or not—that is, when you're dying to get into some special field. Maybe you're so fascinated by the theater that you're willing to be paid peanuts for a chance to breathe dusty backstage air. Or maybe you think you have some special ability in that field.

And you might get somewhere if you're willing, say, to sit at the switchboard of a literary agent whose clients are playwrights, spending your lunch hours poring over plays, scenarios, and so on, and hoping eventually to be asked your opinion. And it does happen. "Take a look at this, and tell me what you think," a play agent said casually one day to a friend of mine who was beginning to droop a little after six months of a switchboard-and-typing job; and he tossed a thick script onto her desk. Since she had been an English and drama major and had been studying plays furiously for the last six months, meanwhile daydreaming of something earth-shaking happening (such as the agent saying casually, "Take a look at this script") she was ready. The door has opened a crack, and next time, maybe *next time*. . . . Well, she won't be the first to work up from switchboard to reader in a playwriting agency, and on into the theatrical excitement.

There are plenty of jobs that fit under the heading of *Exception*. But in some of them you'll need savings or income of your own to piece out your living expenses, unless you're willing to live like one of the poorer of Dickens' characters. High-fashion magazines, for instance, have low-salary budgets, particularly for secretaries (whom they like to be young and personable). If you crave the glamour or chic of being on a high-fashion magazine and you appear to fit the role, you can expect to pay for the glamour by taking home a pittance of a salary. In the lower echelons (it changes later on) you can expect that your raises won't be so much monetary as in being given a fancier title. You graduate from "secretary" to "assistant" or later to "fashion assistant," but when you tear open your pay envelope and find the unchanged tiny sum therein, you can bless the savings that keep you eating decently. I remember once when I worked in the fashion department of a magazine, I secretly paid my secretary an extra sum per week out of my own pocket, out of sheer embarrassment. However, since we are talking about developing yourself as a whole person and having a fine time doing it, there's more than money for you to consider here.

But if you are going to be a *giver* in any of these exception jobs, it is wise to make sure that you are also a *getter*. One woman, an ex-secretary, now in her fifties, about a year ago took a low-paying job with an import-export firm that dealt mostly with France and Italy because she loves the languages and wanted to brush up on her college French and Italian before spending a month's vacation in Europe. She began taking dictation first in French, hardly understanding the words except phonetically, but getting her letters done correctly by constantly referring to her French dictionary. By the time she went abroad eight months later, she was speaking creditable French and an almost fluent Italian. Since she has returned, she is very much a sophisticate about ordering in continental restaurants and she is enjoying reading books and magazines in both languages. Her circle of acquaintances has widened to include Frenchmen and Italians and she is having a fine time. None of this is any surprise to her, since it is really what, she says, "I had in the back of my mind."

Any number of women alone who are rich or have solid incomes are tempted to do volunteer work as a way of "doing something." Besides, it's for humanity isn't it? And unselfish. It is fine to be noble and think of volunteer work and what you can do for humanity. But the way to accomplish most for humanity (and yourself) is to select a volunteer area that is related to your own personality, whether it's working with children, fund-raising, helping the elderly, or whatever, and then boning up on the subject first. Learning anything from the Dewey decimal system of filing, to office management to start with, if you're going to help out in a charitable organization's office, can make your volunteer work worthwhile. Otherwise you'll just be a nuisance, getting in everybody's way—lots of heart-of-gold enthusiasm but as little direction as the man in the Stephen Leacock story who rushed out of the house and "leaped on his horse and galloped off in all directions." Besides, it's more interesting to know the behind-the-scenes problems. Working with the elderly, for instance, takes on an extra dimension when you know something about geriatrics. Working with babies and children is satisfying—but a hundred times more so if you make it your business to know something about pediatrics and child care and child psychology, such as the fact that neglected babies need loving or they begin to suffer from something called "anaclitic depression," from which many of them actually die, whereas holding, loving, and fondling a baby supplies it with a kind of nourishment that helps it to bloom.

When you live alone, you're more liable than other people to the seductive and dangerous attraction of free-lance writing. The situation is ideal, a writer's dream. There you are, an apartment of your own, the luxury of solitude, no family or roommates to interrupt you. You might even travel a little, writing here and there. It sounds like a marvelous life. *Sounds* is the key word. There is a laughable fiction abroad that if you are a writer you gain a coterie of fascinating friends, à la Françoise Sagan or Ernest Hemingway . . . and of course do your writing while this month living in Majorca and next month writing in a hotel room in Paris, Rome, London. I know ordinarily intelligent people who are nevertheless convinced that when you're a writer you meet your fellow writers for coffee and intellectual conversation on weekday afternoons at 4:00 P.M. and who also believe that you are enviably free to go to the beach on weekdays and on shopping trips to department stores at 10:00 o'clock in the morning—all the while producing work that gets you compliments, friends, income, and onto television panel shows.

Writers, even great writers, sometimes believe this kind of fantasy themselves, and some of them even try it after an initial success . . . which is one reason it took F. Scott Fitzgerald seven years to complete *Tender Is the Night*.

In any case, delightful fantasies like this are enough to make anyone consider leaving a job to freelance. The trouble, of course —besides the fact that the fantasy is false—is that writing is probably the loneliest job in existence, if you don't count being a hermit. The live-alone free-lancer spends the entire day in total isolation, without even anyone to knock on the door and say lunch is ready, or later that it's time for dinner. Along with talent, which is basic, you'll need iron discipline if you're going to turn out the work. You'll have to structure your day all by yourself. No shopping trips. No beach, no matter how sunny the day and blue the sky. No afternoon chats with friends, even on the telephone. Otherwise you find yourself insidiously falling into that day-without-structure situation, melting into that jellyfish, complete with anxiety and depression. And of course producing nothing. As one live-alone who was a staff writer on a magazine once explained to me when she cannily decided against free-lancing, "I need some office to go to, somebody to tell me what to do . . . If I free-lanced, I'd lie around all day eating chocolates." And as Bel Kaufman, who wrote *Up the Down Staircase,* put it, "It's so easy *not* to write."

But *if* you can resist the blandishments of sun, friends, and an afternoon nap, or if your creative urge is a vital, important one, then yes, your live-alone life is perfect for free-lance writing. You are free of the thousand daily little jobs of rushing to make beds, fix meals, shop for food. You are free to think, to create. In earlier days, women who became famous in almost any field usually lived alone, or at least weren't married—Jane Austen, Emily Dickinson, Christina Rossetti, Emily Brontë, and others; later, Edna Ferber, Eudora Welty, poet Marianne Moore. Virginia Woolf, in her famous book, *A Room of One's Own,* talking about the need for solitude to write creatively, and about how, in earlier centuries, a woman was cheated of it, wrote, "In the first place, to have a room of her own, let alone a quiet room or a soundproof room, was out of the question, unless her parents were exceptionally rich or very noble, even up to the beginning of the nineteenth century."

But now it is different. A woman can, if she has the desire, talent, and discipline, find her solitude and produce. As Pulitzer Prize-Winning writer Barbara Tuchman (once married, now divorced) once explained, "I can work twelve or more hours a day." And she can sometimes work fifteen hours a day, as she says, "When I'm let alone."

But talent is another thing. And the best way to find out if you have any is to begin writing while working at a writing job on a newspaper or magazine, a trade paper or in an advertising agency —*anywhere* where you'll have to write or can work into a writing job. The next step, if you do have talent, is to keep your creative writing confined to evenings and weekends until you're producing salable enough material to take the risk of leaving a job and earning an income by free-lancing and, of course, until you're confident enough to risk spending your day working in isolation. Even if you're lucky enough to meet anybody but the building superintendent and the waiter in the coffee shop, you'll have to stay away from people and work, at least until you get established. So you had better be sure that you're willing, even delighted, to sacrifice social life and most human contacts, if not forever, for at least a while. To again quote the writer Stephen Leacock, "I am a great believer in luck, and I find the harder I work, the more I have of it."

There are some live-aloners for whom, for one reason or another, a job isn't feasible. If you're among those women, you're going to have to create a backbone for your day if you hope to skirt a Blue Monday state.

Without a job, you can develop passionate interests, you can become involved in helping a political party, you can take a course in anything from botany to medieval literature. You can take advantage of all the free or inexpensive daytime weekday activities.

But the point is to *do* these things. And for that you need a schedule. It doesn't matter what kind of schedule, as long as it gets you up, out, and into action. One of the most successful live-aloners I know is a teacher who retired after thirty years of teaching the history of art. Every morning her alarm clock goes off at 7:30, and she gets up and follows a planned day, already jotted down in advance on her calendar. It might be anything, but it is *specific*. Since she hasn't much money, it is generally free or inexpensive. She has overcome that bugaboo of live-aloners—the uneasy feeling of *I don't want to go alone*. She goes wherever it pleases her to go. Since her main interest is art, she goes to every free art exhibit at galleries and to a museum once a week. She has no painting talent whatsoever, but she attends an art class anyway every Tuesday at 11:00 in the morning, and enjoys it. Tuesday is also the day she eats lunch out in an inexpensive foreign restaurant —Greek, Hungarian, Turkish, Armenian, Czechoslovakian. The foreign-food idea intrigues some of the people she meets in art class and they often accompany her to her foreign lunch. Among the things she has done in the last two months is take a harassed mother's six-year-old son to the Bronx Zoo, and march in a parade to further tenants' rights. She is also fighting to lower the tax rate for single people, so it will be at the same rate as that for married people. Her congressman, at this point, is very much aware of her strong feelings on the single-people tax problem. So are her friends. Altogether, she has managed to put herself across as a concerned human being, and an interesting one, and her telephone rings with amazing frequency. She is never in a deep enough Blue Monday mood to call up people she doesn't really like, just to hear a human voice. To my knowledge, she doesn't ever stop in Schrafft's for coffee and pastry because she has nothing to do . . . though she may stop there to rest her aching feet.

Any schedule, is the idea. It doesn't necessarily have to involve getting up early in the morning—there is no particular virtue in greeting the dawn, and maybe you want to schedule yourself to watch a series of 1920s' movies until 2:00 o'clock in the morning. But the important thing is to have a schedule that includes some kind of self-growth, some passionate interest to follow. Pick one and follow it. There are plenty around, from ecology to music to working to push your present mayor out and a better one in.

One thing that helps to schedule you out of the apartment and into activities is having the right clothes to get out in.

Having only a few attractive but appropriate clothes is ideal: you're freer, more mobile, more likely to want to get out and be seen. Clothes you feel good in can even change your attitude toward life. A few years ago a woman sociologist made a study that fascinated me. She dressed an unbathed and uncombed ten-year-old girl in a shabby, ill-fitting dress and shoes with rundown heels, and sent her out to play. All afternoon as she played the little girl acted sad and mean and angry. The next day the sociologist dressed the same little girl, all scrubbed and scented and with hair brushed to a gloss, in an immaculate and pretty dress and patent leather Mary Janes. And guess what? Do I have to tell you that the little girl metamorphosed into somebody who was eager and happy and delighted with herself, and *interested?*

The fewer clothes, the better, if you want to be more mobile, whether you have a job or not. The most successful wardrobe I know of belongs to a twenty-eight-year-old copywriter in an advertising agency. She lists her essentials as: one expensive suit, a bare handful of slacks and tops, two cocktail dresses, three daytime dresses, a fake fur coat, a light coat, one long evening gown, and one evening stole. She has three purses, five pairs of shoes, three handsome scarves. She can dress in five minutes, slip on the appropriate jewelry and be ready for a formal dinner dance or a walk in the woods. She has a practically empty closet and can put her hand on the right beautiful thing to wear in an instant. She says she got the idea after seeing Audrey Hepburn get dressed in Givenchy clothes in *Breakfast at Tiffany's* in two minutes flat while carrying on a conversation with the young man who lived upstairs.

The reason it is unwise to have frumpy clothes in the closet is that you will wear them. Worse, you might stay home.

CHAPTER 4

The Money Side

The writer and wit, Dorothy Parker, once sighed that "I never expect to become a millionaire—but I think I would be *darling* at it."

I know any number of people who also would be darling at it. But it is true, too, that you can lead an infinitely more darling life on the money you do have, if you know how to handle it. The idea, of course, is to handle it so you get the most out of it.

To achieve this, you may first have to do a little backtracking in your notions about money. If you're one of those women who simply isn't knowledgeable about money, it's time you asked yourself, *Why not?* An amazing number of women, for instance, arrive at the live-alone state with no more than a grasshopper's knowledge of how to manage a salary or income. They may know Yeats's poetry and be an expert on symphonic music and how to make a stuffed lobster or antique a chair. But they haven't any idea what their rent totals per year or how much money they spend a month on liquor or laundry. Plenty of women (I was one of them) arrive at the live-alone state without ever having balanced a checkbook, and even ignorant of the difference between the interest a savings bank pays and what a commercial bank pays. One otherwise intelligent young schoolteacher recently explained to me that she keeps her money in a certain commercial bank "because that's where my grandmother always kept her money." And I know a twenty-eight-year-old publisher's assistant who handles her job competently, but who, when her brother tried to explain to her some simple facts about money, fluttered her hands madly in front of her face, shaking her head and protesting in panic: "I don't want to know!"

This twenty-eight-year-old's protest sounds extreme, but she is not so extreme after all. What she is, like so many of us, is a direct descendant of the endearing-dope-with-a-checkbook tradition. This could otherwise be called the *Life with Father* syndrome. In *Life with Father,* Mother is flutteringly hopeless about money, and we read that "She didn't feel that women should have anything to do with accounts, any more than men should have to see that the parlor was dusted." We read all about her womanly foibles with money, and that Father "Once every month regularly . . . held court and sat as a judge, and required her to explain her crimes and misdemeanors" about money. Father, on the whole, was tolerant, or as tolerant as he could be, when sometimes Mother would put down all sorts of little expenses on the backs of envelopes, and "He would pore over them . . . in a vain attempt to bring order out of this feminine chaos." We read also that Father "said that as he always paid her bills she had no use for money." Naturally, she had no bank account.

Life with Father is a funny book and it is good for any number of laughs and has been reprinted twenty-four times, most recently in 1963, and right now there are doubtless hundreds of women reading it and laughing their heads off. But it is not to our mind so funny about women-and-money, unless you are laughing while at the same time knowing that you are a live-aloner with a comfortable cushion of security and money-knowledge.

Of course there are women who are knowledgeable about financial matters. But most of us suffer to a considerable degree from a *Life with Father* hangover. This may be at least partly why such an astonishing number of widows come to the live-alone state as money-ignorant as Mother in *Life with Father*. Statisticians have estimated that most widows spend at least 80 percent of their lump-sum insurance money within a year after receiving it. Eighty dollars out of each one hundred dollars gone! Disappeared! Melted away! Insurance companies have said they are mystified as to *why*. But one New England economist told me bluntly that the reason is simple: "Most widows don't know beans about money." A good rule for the live-aloner to observe is that if, like Mother, you don't, as they say, "bother your pretty little head" about money, you're liable to find yourself with very little of it to bother about.

Some women would rather not bother their pretty little heads because they feel guilty and uneasy about paying any attention at all to money. They think of money as a masculine province, vaguely equating it with being aggressive or "materialistic." The synonyms for money, such as *filthy lucre* or *dirty money* almost make money sound like something a lady never touched, unless perhaps with gloves on. Some women simply assume that they "have no head for business" or that they "can't handle money." After all, society has told them this for so long that they believe it. Yet little girls are much better at figures and mathematics than little boys—but, say sociologists, very early in school little girls will suddenly freeze and become incompetent with figures, and little boys draw ahead of them. One sociologist explains that little girls become "rattled" when they get the idea that mathematics are for little boys and dolls are for little girls.

It is reassuring to know that you have all the mental equipment you need to take care of your money—the spending of it, the saving of it, the investing of it. It is very important to realize this. Otherwise you will fumble the handling of money (which is costly), and obligingly work for less money (which is costly), and profligately give away your knowledge and time (which is costly).

But it is quite a different story when you know what you're about. I know one enviable California woman who has a ten-room house, a heated swimming pool, a good cook, and a secure life. Nobody left her a dime. She achieved it all by spending four hours each morning going over her investments, made originally with earnings saved from her department-store-buyer job. The rest of the day, she is free to think about other things . . . among them love, literature, and some volunteer work with deaf children. If she did not spend those four hours on "materialistic" things, she could not afford the time to give to love, literature and deaf children. Having to scrimp is time-consuming. The more your uncared-for money dwindles, the more time you're going to have to spend worrying about where to get some of it to pay off a television set, buy a new dress, try to afford a car. I know one twenty-four-year-old painter who is a very good artist indeed, but she scorns being "materialistic" and is inclined to give away her paintings or sell them at ridiculously low prices. She explains that she doesn't like to "think" about money. Consequently, her apartment is cold in winter and suffocatingly hot in summer, and she can't afford to buy the paint and canvases she needs. Sometimes she takes part-time jobs to pay her rent and buy food. Meanwhile her artist friends who demand a decent price for their work have time to paint, and can afford the proper materials, and live comfortably.

Saving money is vital. Savings, when you live alone, are the Gibraltar that will finally provide you with everything from a part-time maid to vintage wine, to travel, if those are your choices. Above all, savings will save you from ever being at such a low financial ebb that you'll have to move in with relatives . . . thereby losing all the live-alone freedom and pleasures you've learned to appreciate.

The only way to save money is to know what you're spending it on. This can turn out to be very difficult. Almost anybody is inclined to resist this knowledge, since facing where our money goes often means facing disagreeable facts. If you have been casual with your money or inclined to be extravagant, you'll be in for any number of disagreeable little shocks. It's no fun, for instance, to see right there, in incontrovertible figures on your desk, that in the last six months you have spent triple what you thought you spent on clothes, and quadruple what you could have sworn you were spending on movies and other entertainment. *Whatever happened to all that money?* is a panicky thought that usually occurs at income tax time; then it drops into the background, almost as if looking back is too risky, as though you could turn into a pillar of salt.

To save, you are going to have to budget. I say "have to" because budgeting is mandatory—just as mandatory as if you were U.S. Steel, which has *its* budget, or General Motors, with *its* budget. It is just as important for you as for General Motors, and even more so, since you live alone, and if you get into financial difficulties you can't file for bankruptcy or sell more stock or scream to the government for help. Also, your aim, like theirs, is to stay in business and show a profit—profit, in your case, is savings. Investing will come later.

You'll feel better about budgeting along with General Motors if you keep reminding yourself that your savings will do more than secure your future—they will also give you more freedom, the power of choice: to switch jobs, to move to another city, to make opportune investments, to live half the year in the South of France if you feel like it.

Budgeting is, simply, planning ahead. One primer-simple method is to list your expenses for the coming year. You can go by your last year's expenses—what you paid for rent, telephone, annual medical check-up, hairdresser per month, taxes, and so on. That way, after you add up the expenses, you'll only need to divide by twelve to find out what it costs you a month to live. The results can be so astronomical that you may wonder where you got enough money in the first place to pay for all that.

What's more, what with steady inflation, you can generally estimate that it's going to cost you a bit more to live next year than last year. Once you get used to this unappetizing thought, you begin to see where you might make some adjustments. The adjustments, oddly enough, can open up some areas of pleasure. I have one friend who cut out her extravagant habit of taking taxis and spent half the money saved on a long ski weekend in Vermont and banked the other half at 5 percent interest. You may decide that your laundry bill is needlessly high, and save money by going to the laundromat; if you discover that your entertaining includes buying a bottle of Scotch a month, you can save a tidy sum by buying a case of it for your year's supply. Perhaps you're entertaining too expensively and really could use some of that entertainment money for a winter coat, and save the rest. Your guests might be just as happy with a casserole as an expensive cut of beef.

It pays to be businesslike about a budget, not to mention honest with yourself. If you don't like the figures on the desk and start juggling them to make them look better, you'll only be pasting yourself into a financial corner. It may be cheering to estimate that you spend only twenty-five dollars a week for groceries when you really suspect you spend fifty dollars, because that leaves you with the illusion that you have twenty-five dollars more for entertainment. But it also leaves you, eventually, in trouble. "I never buy any clothes," a woman friend tells me, and she really believes it is true. "I always do my own hair," another friend says with satisfaction, and so she does—except for her haircuts and styling and occasional special occasions, and the time last year when she wanted streaks. I can remember, during the first year of my budget, telephoning a department store to get an explanation for a puzzling bill, and being told it was for cosmetics. Cosmetics? *Me?* . . . when I buy cosmetics only occasionally, and in a drugstore? Or so I had been telling myself.

A good idea is to pay everything possible by check—rent, Christmas presents, doctors' bills, TV repairs, liquor, dry cleaning—so you will have an *incontrovertible* record. No wishful estimates. Of course this is difficult with food, but one solution is to cash, say, a fifty-dollar check for food, keep it in a separate purse for grocery shopping, and see how long it lasts. You have only to look in your checkbook to see how many fifty-dollar checks a year you use for food. If you have a job, which means lunching out, you can easily keep a one-month record of what you're spending (including tips), and that will give you an idea of your year's lunch expenses.

Having a special checking account generally costs ten cents a check, with a seventy-five-cent monthly charge, but it's priceless at keeping you posted as to where your money goes. Or you can have a *regular* checking account, and thereby not pay anything for your checks. In some banks you can have a regular checking account provided you keep a minimum balance of one hundred dollars to two hundred dollars in your checking account. Others insist on a minimum of three hundred dollars or even five hundred dollars. Banks are so eager for your patronage that some of them lately offer you a free checking account for a whole year if you'll only be so good as to open a savings account of a couple of hundred dollars in their bank.

Wherever your money *does* go—whether you decide on the extravagance of having an expensive car and are therefore willing to live in a smaller apartment, or however you want to economize in one place to afford something else—there are certain budgeted expenses a live-aloner should regard as sacrosanct. One is adequate health insurance, unless you're so preposterously rich that you can snap your fingers at the idea of tremendous hospital and doctors' bills wiping out your savings (I don't know anybody that rich). You also need insurance against theft, fire, and accidents. A vacation is another necessary expense, since everybody needs one. The fourth, of course, is savings, savings for emergencies and for investments for your future security and for current extras like a fur hat, an art book, an apartment with a fireplace.

Being businesslike about a budget also means having a file, even if it's a small one on a table in the corner of your bedroom, in which you have folders that suit your life—a folder on taxes, a folder containing guarantees on things you buy (like a hair dryer, a camera, an electric toothbrush, a clock radio, an exercise bicycle), a Christmas folder (presents, card list), parties you gave (what you spent for food and liquor for each party and what you bought), an investment folder (even if you are buying one bond a month or have one share of stock). If it is sailboats you love and spend money on, you need a sailboat file. If you have a car, what do you spend on it? Your car file will deliver the information.

You can become quite an expert at saving in lots of small ways —as is a ballet teacher I know who lives in a chic apartment despite a small income, yet saves money with the ease of Aladdin rubbing a magic lamp. She watches the *little* things. When she went on a diet and bought a blender she consulted *Consumers' Reports* at her neighborhood library (where she also reserves good new books and best sellers), and she does the same thing for whatever appliance she buys. When she makes a telephone call and gets a wrong number, she is not shy about calling the operator and getting credit for it. She buys a year's supply of food staples at a time, as though she were setting off on a trip to the Klondike. She does this whenever buying in quantity is less expensive. She puts what she saves into a good growth stock, reinvests all the dividends, and is a little surprised herself at how well she is doing. She's about thirty-eight, and has been reinvesting for a few years now, so she's bound to have a comfortable income if she doesn't marry, and a nice nest egg if she does.

Budgeting and money may at first give you a hearty headache and be depressing besides. But once it begins to make sense, you may even become fascinated by it. Lots of women do. Shirley MacLaine, actress who is now also a successful movie producer, not long ago commented that "I really enjoy knowing how money works." Miss MacLaine never went to college, but that didn't hinder her from finding out about money and developing an unerring eye for costs. "I know how to read budgets," Miss MacLaine explained recently in discussing her success as a producer. "In fact I can tell from reading a book how much the adaptation will cost." Shrewd movie magnates here and in England now bow to Miss MacLaine's financial judgments, and when she wants anybody to invest a million dollars, she has only to say so in order to get it.

No one, of course, not Miss MacLaine or anyone, pulls money-knowledge out of a hat. You have to develop your knowledge, you have to pay attention to your money affairs. *And you have to keep the guiding reins in your own hands.* No one—not your accountant (if you have one) or your lawyer (if you have one) or your ex-husband's best friend, or that nice man at the bank with the twinkly eyes, or anyone else—can be responsible for taking over and running your finances. It is your money and you care about it more than they do. Besides, all these gentlemen may be willing and goodhearted and honest (if you're lucky) but not necessarily competent. Plenty of women alone have been the victims not of nefarious plots, but rather, of well-meaning uncles and other relatives who misjudged the stock market or really believed in other disastrous investments they recommended. I know a widow who put all her insurance money into her brother-in-law's new ice-cream-manufacturing business, and all she ended up with a year later was all the ice cream she could eat. With a little practice, you can become reasonably competent at judging how to invest your money, and you needn't take anybody else's word for it.

Besides, when you're in charge of your own finances, you get a nice feeling of security by knowing *exactly* where you stand financially, any week, any month. It's your own show. And you're running it. It also helps you gain a sense of "place" in this economic world.

That doesn't mean you shouldn't ask people's advice. But it should be professional advice from people such as accountants and investment counselors and other professionals. You want knowledgeable advice on money matters, and professionals can widen your knowledge. "Security," someone once said, "is having a good analyst, lawyer, doctor, and accountant." Easy if you're rich. Otherwise, you should at least discuss your taxes and budget with an accountant—which is one way to get to afford the analyst, lawyer, and doctor. What you pay the accountant can pay off handsomely in the money he saves you. But even if you have an accountant make out your income tax, it is worth it to discuss and to study what he figured and why, and to understand the results thoroughly, rather than just signing the papers and sending them off. That's part of your money education.

There are any number of places to put your savings so that, as time passes, you'll have the satisfaction of knowing that you're getting richer by the hour, the day, the year.

Banks are generally safe, barring such exceptional disasters as the 1930s' bank closing. Besides, banking your money is better than hiding it in a suitcase in the closet or under your scarves in a bureau drawer, since the bank pays interest and the bureau drawer does not. Besides, money in a bureau drawer shrinks, because of inflation, so the money is worth less as time goes on.

But while banks pay interest, some categories of banks pay more interest than others. So it's wise to check which bank will pay you the most on your savings, until you get around to thinking about investing it. Since January 1971, commercial banks are allowed by the government to pay as high as 4½ percent interest on your savings account. But you can get up to 5 percent from a savings and loan association bank or a mutual savings bank. If you can't find a bank in your neighborhood that pays 5 percent, it's perfectly legal for you to bank by mail, in a faraway town or city. Banks are usually so delighted to have you as a patron that they pay the round-trip postage.

Whatever bank you pick for your savings, you'd better make sure it's a member of the FDIC, which is the Federal Deposit Insurance Corporation. That means that your money will be insured up to twenty thousand dollars in case of some incomprehensible disaster like the earlier-mentioned Roosevelt closings of the 1930s. If you have more than twenty thousand dollars in a FDIC member bank, talk to the manager about the best way to spread the money in different accounts so it will *all* be insured. After all, the only reason you're keeping money in a bank at all is to make more money, not take risks, no matter how outlandish or unlikely they seem.

Depending on how often you deposit and withdraw money during the month, you may be better off with a "day of deposit" account instead of a "regular" savings account—and it is checking little things like this that add up to more interest and a bigger security cushion for you. So it is worth discussing your particular deposit and withdrawal habits with the bank teller—even a half-dozen times if necessary—until the better choice for you is clear in your mind.

Also, if you have five hundred dollars or more in the bank and you honestly know you won't have to touch it, a bank will pay you anywhere from ½ percent to 1 percent a year *more* interest if you agree not to withdraw that sum for a certain period of time, usually thirty days to a year. So you'll be getting up to 6 percent interest on your money. You tie up your five hundred dollars or whatever by opening what's called a Time-Deposit Account or by buying Certificates of Deposit, which are about the same thing. Some banks offer more interest than others on these accounts, so it's worth it to shop around. A dress designer friend of mine shifted her saved-up lump sum of $4,000 from one bank Time-Deposit Account to another and thereby got ¾ percent more interest, which was at least enough to buy her a season ticket to the Philharmonic, with some money left over.

If you're the kind of person whose money seems to evaporate on the way to the bank, you'll need outside discipline to help you save. You're better off turning to what people call "forced savings" —committing yourself to a mutual fund or an annuity, so that you have to pay a certain sum a month toward your future, very much like Christmas Club savings, except that that particular Christmas will come twenty or thirty or forty years from now, and what with interest and dividends it will be quite a windfall. It will be nice to know that when you're no longer getting a paycheck you'll be getting a regular check anyway. It is rather like inheriting money, except that you're the one who leaves the money to yourself. There is nothing like having a solidly secure income, a fact that writer Virginia Woolf commented on very movingly when, never having had any money, and having to scrape along on tiny jobs, she was left five hundred pounds a year—in those days about two thousand dollars—through a legacy from an aunt. "No force in the world," said Miss Woolf, almost in disbelief, in discussing that event, "can take from me my five hundred pounds. Food, house and clothing are mine for ever."

Then there is the stock market with "safe" stocks and with stocks as speculative as playing Russian roulette. Unless you want to take a course in economics (which I will discuss in a few moments) *or* are willing to bone up on the market and watch daily newspaper stock reports and spend time keeping a close eye on your investments, you're better off with safe stocks. That is, stocks that earn money year in and year out and that pay you dividends regularly every three months. Safe? *How* safe? Investing in the market is a risk, but the New York Stock Exchange actually does list 627 common stocks that have been paying, at this writing, at least one cash dividend regularly, every quarter. Three of these have done so *for more than one hundred years,* so you're not living particularly dangerously by buying them. Eleven others have paid regular dividends for seventy-five to ninety-nine years . . . 95 have paid regular dividends for fifty to seventy-four years . . . 358 stocks for twenty-five to forty-nine years. And 160 for twenty to twenty-four years. The list is available from the New York Stock Exchange or you can get it from any New York Stock Exchange member firm in your city. But keep in mind that these stocks don't necessarily pay a high dividend. If you buy them, you will be safe and not sorry, but you also won't become a Croesus.

If you're willing to spend the time to do better than that in the stock market, it won't hurt to spend an evening a week taking a course and learning some basics about investing. You might even discover you have a desire to go really deeply into the money game, as happened to a young English teacher I know who took an investment analysis course at Bernard Baruch College. She became so enamored of finance that she eventually switched to a job in Wall Street. Four years ago she passed her brokerage exams and now at the age of thirty-one is a registered stockbroker with her own clients at the Wall Street firm where she works. She reads the *New York Times* financial section at breakfast, and the *Wall Street Journal* on the subway, and she spends lunchtime at the stock exchange. Her idea of a good time is to spend hours chatting with stockbrokers about money (which is not such a bad way to spend your time, at that). She is also in a perfect position to invest knowledgeably and she loves the business. I also know a twenty-eight-year-old legal secretary from Colorado who fell in love with finance, took two economics courses at night, and is now an assistant to an investment counselor in a Denver bank. Her job doesn't hurt her investments or her social life, either. Just as people at parties always ask psychiatrists about emotional problems and doctors about physical problems, they ask investment counselors about their financial ones. Men never used to cluster around this young woman investment counselor in the days when she was a legal secretary.

It won't hurt, either, if you take up money as a hobby, like stamp-collecting or bird-watching. It can be as fascinating as any other hobby, and more so, since it involves human beings, international affairs, domestic politics, and your own comfort and security. Browsing in the economics section of the library, you can find books on money management, accounting for beginners, economics-for-living, and other money subjects. If you want to explore more deeply, you can take courses in real estate, banking, and so on. Even dipping into a subject for three months can orient you financially. When you pick investments, you might as well pick those that give you some extra pleasure. Why not, if you like travel, invest in a travel agency? Why not, if you like the shore, invest in an ocean-resort development? If you're keen for photography, why not a photography stock? I know a woman who just a few years ago lived well, even fashionably, in a New York apartment, hating every minute of it, but tied to the city by her job as a department-store executive. She had grown up in the country, and her concept of happy living centered around under-the-trees picnics, biting into October apples, and walking in the woods in spring. One boring Saturday she dropped into a bookstore where she aimlessly picked up a book. It was about land investment, and she read the whole thing through while standing right there. She then bought the book and took it home. Some three months later, she invested in a wild, tree-covered, eight-acre wilderness with a fresh, wide brook, just a two-hour ride into the country. She now picnics there weekends with freinds, eats October apples, and takes country walks in the spring. She owns only a ten-by-twelve screened house on the property, to keep off the rain and keep out the mosquitoes. Meanwhile her property keeps increasing in value at a rate that astonishes her. She receives excellent offers to sell, which she politely turns down, and her accountant tells her that her investment is safer and more valuable than almost any other type of investment she could have made.

Whether you're going to put your money into raising dogs

or into an annuity, or real estate, or whether you're simply trying to get by on your salary and save ten dollars a week for now, an aim is important: a direction. What you do with your money is wholly your own affair; you can plan your expenses and your savings to suit yourself, but you should plan with *something in mind*.

More, never never assume that because you live alone, you have to "make do" instead of aiming to live better, more comfortably, more elegantly if you choose, and with more assurance. So if you have not, as they say, been "bothering your pretty little head" about money-knowledge, the sooner you do the more advantages you will have. I have an almost mystical respect for a friend of mine who, when told by a rather smug acquaintance that "Money can't buy happiness," answered that maybe not but in any case she would rather cry herself to sleep on a silk pillow.

CHAPTER 5

Where to Live: City? Country? Suburbs?

There is an old comic routine that goes "Are you having any fun?" If the answer that springs to mind is "Not much," where you live could be partly responsible. There are, for instance, any number of women who are divorced, widowed, or otherwise alone, and who are still living where they just happened to be living when their circumstances changed and they found themselves alone. They might be having a considerably better time elsewhere.

Living in the suburbs by yourself can be as lonely as being on a raft in mid-ocean, and lonelier than Napoleon on Elbe. That's particularly true if your suburban married friends have a two-by-two social attitude, so that you're odd woman out. It is no news that a suburban live-aloner's social life can dwindle down to evenings of looking at television or taking a lonely Saturday ride in the car if she has a car. One particularly gregarious new widow I know stood it for six months before she rented her house, sold her car, and moved into the city where she has the advantage of getting to her job in a flat ten minutes, and a choice of a couple of dozen other single people with whom she can go to the movies or out to dinner. Not to mention the dozens of places she can go on her own.

This is not a polemic against the suburbs in favor of city living. What I mean to say here is that, living alone, you're more mobile: you're free to make any number of choices about where you want to live. Some places are bound to be more soul-satisfying than others. It doesn't matter where you choose to live—city, country, suburbs, or even on a houseboat (I know somebody who chose exactly that)—as long as the place suits your taste and supplies at least some friends and social activity, and, unless you have an income, a means of making a living.

But sometimes, under some circumstances, it is wiser to move. Here, for example, is a widow friend of mine who was living in a pleasant New England town when her husband died. She had a house full of fond memories and an attic full of sentimental mementos, and she couldn't visualize living elsewhere. But the house was so big that it took her two days a week to clean it (she no longer could afford a maid), the taxes were high, and what with heat and electric bills, the house was eating up the insurance money her husband had left, plus the small salary she was earning at the local hosiery shop. Besides, in her age group—she was forty-nine—there were three women to every man in town and the men were all thoroughly married. Yet she felt "stuck," unable to move. Where would she go, what would she do? The only other place to live in town was a boardinghouse that was as peaceful as the grave, which was a little too peaceful for her. What finally roused her was her depleted bank account and a week in bed with a slipped disc acquired from mowing the half-acre of lawn. She decided that her few old friends weren't worth this high price, and neither was her job. She put the money-devouring house on the market, had a garage sale, and sold off the attic mementos for a surprisingly large sum. She then moved to New Orleans where she has a handful of relatives, the kind of relatives who "know everybody." She now also knows everybody, has a job in a stocking shop, and for the first time in four years is able to buy herself some new clothes to meet the "everybody" in.

Is this the life I really want? is the question to ask yourself when it comes to thinking: Shall I stay? Or go? You'll have to consider whether you're really stuck where you are . . . what, for instance, is holding you? Is it worth it? A job is often replaceable elsewhere, and sometimes instead of a new job you can get a job transfer to another city or town.

If, for instance, you're the kind of person who feels hemmed in, culturally or socially, by small town or suburban living, what's to stop you from departing for the city, with its wider horizons? Or if you're new to the suburbs—one of the thousands of secretaries, career women, teachers living in the suburbs because it's cheaper—and you're commuting to a job in the city, you may want to reconsider your choice. I know a dozen secretaries in their twenties and thirties who live in a state of suspended social animation, like puppets on frozen strings, once they get home to their apartment in the suburbs. Pretty trees, but no place to go. Fresh air, but how exciting can a trip to the laundromat be? For them, there are no occasional evenings of companionship, nobody to take an hour's stroll with, no friends to confide in and to trade opinions and gossip with over a cocktail or a coffee-and-sandwich visit. Of course, if you can't live happily without trees in plain sight, that's one thing. Or you may have another reason for being crazy about the suburbs. I know a tennis-playing secretary who lives in suburban Forest Hills and that, to her, is heaven. But if it is only a low rent you're after, and you're lonely, you might consider sacrificing your three-and-a-half-room spacious suburban apartment for a cramped one-and-a-half city domicile, where the companionship of more friends can be worth it. And it is hackneyed but true that men have an unconscious (or conscious) resistance to dating someone who has to be taken home to the suburbs at midnight.

Conversely, you may be living in the city and wishing you were elsewhere. A successful elderly publicist friend of mine who lived in a New York apartment on a traffic-noisy street, began to yearn for the seashore and tranquility. On the very week of her retirement she moved to a snug house on Cape Cod. There she now lives, all year round, except for summers, when she rents the house for six weeks and goes to Ireland with a friend, to escape the tourist crowds. The summer rental brings her fifteen hundred dollars and it costs her five hundred dollars to vacation in Ireland (including her round-trip excursion fare). The one thousand dollars she has left goes for groceries and taxes on the house. She has made friends with several other women alone (she calls them "loners") on the Cape, and they all seem to have a very good time, gardening, visiting, and occasionally driving up to Boston to the theater. . . . Another escapee from the city is a thirty-year-old magazine writer friend of mine, a zesty, outdoor type who hated her city life. She finally saved up enough for a down payment on a small house in a rural part of Connecticut. Her outdoor activities involve everything from raising tomatoes to spending weeks laying a brick patio off her kitchen. Friends and relatives had warned her that her move to the country would be financially unwise because she wouldn't be able to spend so much time seeing magazine editors, and her business contacts would fade away. She admits she now has a high telephone bill for long distance calls to editors, and it costs her several dollars to take the train to the city once a month to maintain business contacts, but on the other hand, it costs her far less to live in the country and life is infinitely pleasanter. Surprisingly, she finds the country less lonely than the city, since her city friends are very eager to drive out to the country for a dinner of barbecued hamburgers and fresh-grown vegetables, or to spend a lazy weekend. They generally come bearing gifts of Scotch, gin, and wine in such quantities that she is storing it in a closet and thinking of giving it back to them for Christmas.

If you get satisfaction out of being a big frog in a little puddle, a small town is a good puddle to be in, provided you're willing to put in some effort. I know one big-city widow who felt that way, and who packed up and moved to a middle-Atlantic town where she is now supremely happy. She hates physical activity but she loves the countryside and wants to preserve it so she has got herself elected to the town zoning board. She gets a pittance for holding a minor town office, and her small house on a tarred road is the scene of at least two evening meetings a week in front of her fireplace, involving town affairs. I would say she is approximately as busy as the governor of her state, and certainly a lot happier and more appreciated.

But you had better allow for your own temperament, your own idiosyncrasies, in choosing where to live, once you're alone. It doesn't make much sense to go on living in a country house or rattling around in a big suburban home that once housed your entire family, if you're a timid person. Most people who live in country or suburban houses stubbornly insist they're as safe as living in any city apartment. They could be right, but a lot of good that will do you if you're going to lie in bed at night, quaking and waiting for a creak on the stairs. Timidity can be a genuinely good reason for selling the house you're living in—and it is an equally good reason not to be captured by the looks of a pretty little house that cries out to be bought or rented. What looks bucolic and delightful in full daylight can be more Bela Lugosi at night if you are a nervous type.

If you pine for the exhilarating smog-filled air of cities, pick the city with care. Some cities are so costly that unless you are transferring to a well-paying job you can find yourself living on rice and cabbage and with too little money for clothes, entertainment, going out with new friends to enjoy the city restaurants, and so on. The twelve most expensive cities in the United States are Anchorage, Honolulu, New York, Boston, Cleveland, Hartford, Buffalo, Milwaukee, San Francisco, Chicago, Washington, Seattle. If what they offer strikes you as absolutely necessary to your happiness, go ahead.

Once you get there, even the smallest studio apartment is an infinitely better choice than some kind of women's residence. Living in a women's club or hotel kills your social life right out of hand, since you're not allowed to entertain friends, and consequently you yourself will seldom be entertained. Besides, a few weeks of inhabiting one of those cramped, colorless cubicles, and you'll feel like a combination overage Girl Scout and over-the-hill college graduate, and you might as well be back where you weren't having much fun in the first place.

Even a one-room-and-kitchenette apartment becomes your home, a real home that you can make into something charming and comfortable and distinctly reflecting your personality. And of course you'll be able to entertain all you want, even flambéing oranges in brandy to your heart's content, without worrying about a desk clerk downstairs calling up and saying he smells smoke.

Wherever you do live, it should suit your personality, or the result is gloom and disaster. It was both of these for a forty-two-year-old English teacher friend of mine who transferred from a small California town to Los Angeles and moved into a huge, beautiful, new "singles" apartment complex. The complex was complete with exercise room, sauna bath, outdoor swimming pool shaped like a fish, and it teemed with single people. Since my friend didn't know anyone at all in Los Angeles, the apartment complex sounded ideal. Built-in friends! The trouble was that she hated exercise, the sun gives her brown spots (which eliminated sitting around the pool), and she found no friends with whom she had interests in common, such as reading aloud from her favorite poets. Worse, the single men were much younger than she had expected and even the older ones seemed to be looking over her head at pretty girls in the elevator. She found herself in a constant state of embarrassment, and at night she would lie sleepless in bed, listening to the sounds of parties in a half-dozen apartments around hers, and feeling rejected. After three wretched months she sublet the apartment to a twenty-six-year-old secretary who is outgoing, meets people easily, laughs a lot, spends her free time tanning at the swimming pool, and is probably having a splendid time. My teacher friend moved into a pleasant walk-up apartment on a tree-lined street. Having nothing to do with her evenings, she began moonlighting by teaching English literature night classes. She now has a favorite pupil who is a chemical engineer five years older than she, and who shares her literary interests, very often over dinner in her apartment. Some of her new friends even think he lives there.

If you've been assuming that being an older woman rules out living adventurously, you are mistaken. Adventure seems to catch on with lots of live-aloners when they get older and have the income to satisfy a taste for action. A recent newspaper story, for instance, concerns a woman from Columbus, Ohio, who says, "I'll be seventy-four first thing you know," and who travels by car-and-trailer eight months of the year. She is a widow who retired from her stenography job ten years ago, bought her trailer for ten thousand dollars, and took off. She belongs to a caravan club, and in the last ten years she's traveled to Hawaii, Alaska, all the other states and Canada, and to Mexico six times, in the company of other trailers. Her favorite activity is going on a six-week international rally of her caravan club, and plans are in the offing for trailer-camping through Europe. She says she usually likes to take an "older" woman along with her on her travels, on the off-chance that she might get lonely, and to help with expenses. Ten years ago this style of living was practically unheard of, but now plenty of older women (and men) have decided it's more fun than being stationary. In fact, last I heard, there were 120 chapters of this particular caravan club across the country.

Whether you decide it suits you to live adventurously (or what's the fun?) or you choose to settle down snugly in a suburban garden apartment to a life as peaceful as a Bach fugue, reading library books, having a few friends, and playing tennis on free courts, you can always change your mind. After all, you're not pinned to that particular life just because you've chosen it. And even a small income generally allows room for two or more choices.

Since you have the whole say about how you spend your money, go ahead and have the pleasure of splitting your living expenses as eccentrically as you like. Odd as your style of living may strike other people, do it anyway. . . . I commend one nervy young divorcée for bravery in doing just that. Newly divorced and about to open a small boutique near Chapel Hill, North Carolina, she needed a place to live. One possibility she went to look at was a house outside of town, a small rectangular cinderblock house that had been built for eleven thousand dollars and a big oval-shaped swimming pool that had cost eight thousand dollars. House and pool were connected by a dilapidated trellis of scrawny rambler roses, and the property was being sold dirt-cheap by a swimming pool company that had built and used it for advertising purposes, and who figured that it would have to go that cheap because who would be so foolish . . . ? The divorcée visualized the pool painted lime green, the house whitewashed, the trellis blooming with masses of red roses, and decided *she* was that foolish. Her bank regarded the project as a poor investment, but she was able to borrow the money elsewhere. On her part it turned out to be an excellent investment. She and her odd and pretty domicile now attract people like honey the bears, her boutique business benefits from the reflected glamour, and she is regarded as a person of imagination and style, which she is.

CHAPTER 6

Creating the Personal Background

No matter how often you go out, you eventually have to come home. Obviously, then, you need a home you can love to come home to. Especially when you're going to be there a lot.

Your apartment (which it usually is) should give you as much of a warm glow as a glass of good wine. The idea of being snowed in by a blizzard for three days should strike you as delightful. More, your bedroom should please you so much that you hate to turn out the light and go to sleep. *That's* the apartment you want—a place that is so soul-satisfying that you can enjoy whatever evenings and weekends you spend alone. Besides that, it should be a place where you can entertain easily and happily. The size of your place needn't hold you back. A one-room-and-kitchenette apartment can have as much charm and chic and comfort as a Park Avenue duplex—and often it has more.

It helps enormously if you go on the assumption that nothing is too good for you. A dilapidated chair in a mud-colored slipcover is not good enough for you. Neither is an Indian cotton bedspread left over from college days. Seedy furnishings like this only irritate and depress you, whereas an I-deserve-the-best philosophy leads to creating the kind of inviting, refreshing surroundings that are wonderful for your morale. Besides, as I suggested earlier, how you treat yourself influences how other people will treat you—and your apartment gives you away immediately: dreary furnishings telegraph the instant news that that's what you think is good enough for you, but charming surroundings convey the news that you think you deserve the best; consequently you're more likely to get it.

Style and charm are important, and you don't need a millionaire's budget to achieve them, either. A few years ago, if you couldn't afford expensive, elegant surroundings, you were stuck with dowdy or fake-something. Now your guests can loll on chairs blown up with a bicycle pump if that's your taste; if you like a French country look you can do effective things with inexpensive toile lamps, paint, mural wallpaper, and you can antique a second-hand breakfront with a kit. Whatever your age, or whatever image you want to create for yourself, you can do it without spending a sum of money that makes you tense to think about. I know a boutique owner in her thirties whose living room is enviable—and inexpensive; it has brilliant pink cushions strewn over two black-and-white flowered sofas, a mushroom-shaped wicker hassock she painted pink, a white-painted coffee table (which she cut down from a mahogany Salvation Army library table), a scattering of bird prints (she framed them herself) matted in green on the white walls, and little else—except lots of popularity. It all looks fresh as apple blossoms. A current magazine says that you can furnish a living room for one thousand dollars, but I happen to know that my boutique-owner friend spent less than that.

Style. *Your* style. A big step toward achieving your own style is to clear your apartment of all the gifts and heirlooms that don't suit your personality. It never pays to hold onto anything you don't honestly like. Just because your aunt crocheted that puce-colored pillow with her own hands is no excuse for keeping it. You don't need it any more than you need a moose head on your wall. Solving the gift problem can, admittedly, be a traumatic experience, as it was with a friend of mine whose father gave her an expensive heirloom crystal chandelier that looked ridiculous in her beloved, peasant-type Italian country living room; it took several months, dozens of tranquilizers, and two psychiatric consultations before she eventually shipped it back to him. But you have to face it, steel yourself, and do what's necessary: after all *you* live there.

As for heirlooms, they're only worth the pleasure they give you. And sometimes they even give you subliminal pain. Once, visiting a friend, I happened to mention that an English Toby jug that sat on top of a bookcase had pretty colors, to which she replied vehemently that she hated it. It turned out that she'd had that antique jug for eight years, and it reminded her of a particular fat and unfriendly English cousin she disliked. Why hadn't she got rid of it? Well, it was valuable and . . . well, she'd never thought about it, though she felt vaguely depressed whenever she happened to glance at it. . . . Now with her eyes newly opened, she looked around the room and announced that she hated—had hated since childhood, in fact—an ugly sideboard her mother had sent her, yet she'd never thought of discarding it. Within the next hour she had listed the Toby jug, the sideboard, an end table, a rocker, and three china dishes with Dresden shepherdesses on them to offer an antique dealer. And for the first time she was excited about the possibility of a room she really liked taking shape.

Expensive mistakes you've bought are sometimes the hardest to part with, since they're an admission of money ill spent, and you hate to think you were ever such an idiot. Part with them anyway if they're wrong. Like the heirlooms, they don't do a thing for your emotional state, and they spoil the room for you.

If you've moved from a larger home to a smaller one, as so many widows and divorcées do, you may have some hulking pieces of furniture that dwarf your smaller apartment rooms like owls in a canary cage. Call the thrift shop or a secondhand dealer, or somebody, anybody, but get rid of them. Moving out an overstuffed elephant of a chair can make room for two smaller comfortable chairs that are in scale with the room. Selling a big table that looked fine in the dining room of a country house can free a whole living-room wall you really need for a couch.

That doesn't mean you should banish antiques or oddities you love—I know a woman who moved from the country to a small city apartment and brought with her a seated stone dog four feet high, a graceful whippet she couldn't part with. She had no room for stone whippets in her living room, so she painted it white, garlanded its neck with blue forget-me-nots (fake) and stood it in her tiny hallway where it guards the door, looks sensational, and delights visitors.

Besides, as everybody knows, a fusty piece of furniture that strikes a wrong note is often worth converting. Most people lately are great converters, and some of them convert ugly ducklings into swans with considerable style and verve. "I can't wait until my sofa arrives," a twenty-two-year-old American history major told me, after her family had promised to send her an old, faded plush Victorian couch for her studio apartment. When it arrived she upholstered it in fake zebra and painted the frame white; then she set a tub of tropical greenery beside it, and over it she hung framed sepia pictures of Teddy Roosevelt in his African hunting days. It's now a main attraction in her apartment and a starting point for all kinds of Rooseveltiana conversations.

Any one-woman ménage (or any other kind) is bound to cost some money, but it costs a lot less if you take the trouble to learn how to go about achieving satisfying effects. Haunting a few showrooms is helpful. So is lifting ideas from friends you visit or wherever else you spot them, culling left and right, jotting down ideas. I remember once stopping at an inn in Portugal and spending the night in an unforgettably beautiful room . . . yet all that really made it outstanding was dark wooden chairs, whitewashed walls, and a lamp shining down on hot-colored cushions on a purple bedspread. You can learn how to use color, lighting, fabrics for all kinds of marvelous, aesthetic effects. I have one friend who, until she could afford a rug for her small foyer, painted an enchanting Turkish one on the floor, complete with fringe. It so delighted visitors that she never did buy a real rug.

Color is such a brightener of moods that while you're donating things you hate to the Salvation Army with one hand (and getting a tax deduction), you might use the other to pick up all sorts of second-hand furniture and paint it to stunning effect. You might do this even if you can afford new furniture; there's a lot to be said for the satisfaction of, say, picking up a pair of battered old Duncan Phyfe reproduction chairs with curved arms for six dollars each, painting them fire-hydrant yellow, upholstering the seats with orange-and-yellow fabric, and using them in a sunny corner of the living room, as I once did. One thing to be said for painting furniture to your own taste is that it is uniquely your own, which is another reason it is a lot more satisfying than just being extravagant.

Keep your extravagances where they count—in a lusciously thick bedroom carpet; in bunches of flowers for your own enjoyment when you're alone instead of only when you have guests; in a bed so fabulous in looks and comfort that you can't wait to get into it. Extravagance where it counts means having cutlery that cuts, a sofa that lasts, the Sunday morning papers delivered.

You can generally improve any room by pruning out clutter, though this is not always true. I have a friend who says "I like too much furniture in a room"—and she jams her living room with fascinating knickknacks, from a collection of snuffboxes to snapshots of men in bowler hats. Visitors enjoy it because they feel (I do, I know) that there's a lot to explore, always something you haven't noticed before. But this is a trick that demands plenty of knowledge. And money. Here is where another kind of extravagance comes in, a kind of *object* extravagance. If you like that sort of thing and can afford it and it's a trick you want to pull off, then dip into the connoisseur types of magazines and read books on various kinds of collecting. You can find books on everything from antique French buttons to Spanish porcelain figures to early American bottles. Movies are a help, too—I know one woman who's been to see *Death in Venice* four times just to study why the hotel tables at the *Hôtel des Bains* look so beautiful with their masses of flowers and small objects.

The less modest you are about expressing your personality, the better. If you can play the piano, have a piano by hook or crook, even a second-hand one. If you like to sketch, frame your sketches and hang them. If you like needlepoint, make the most magnificent-looking cushions in existence. These are all forms of exhibitionism, but what better place to show off than in your apartment? Your personality will be an open secret to whoever enters your house, anyway, so make the most of it.

When you do show off, show off honestly, not pretentiously, since nothing is worse than pretension except being found out. It is no good trying to impress anyone by, for instance, keeping super-intellectual magazines on your coffee table if you really like science fiction, murder mysteries, and gardening-made-easy books; sooner or later this or that guest will glance into your bedroom and spot your real reading on your bedside table.

Whether you want to call them conveniences or comforts, you need certain things. One is a desk. It can be elegant or rococo, English kidney or Directoire, Italian or Moroccan, just so long as it has style and plenty of room for you to write letters and checks. Keep it in the living room if you have to, keep it in a foyer, keep it in the bedroom, but *have* it. Have it with a pretty chair and a good-looking lamp, and with all the paraphernalia like stamps, envelopes, pens, pencils, and perhaps a silver or crystal paperweight to hold down letters. It is an unbelievable convenience that saves all kinds of time and confusion, and it contributes to the apartment's style if it's where it can be seen, and to your own feeling of style if it isn't.

When you live alone it isn't a bad idea to think of yourself as the fairy-tale princess with the pea: anything but the most luxurious makes you black-and-blue. Pampering never hurt anyone. If you like to read in bed, have a padded headboard and a good light to read by; if you like a late-night snack in the living room, why not have a hot plate, perhaps a pretty ceramic one, to keep a teapot hot? When you think of it, most Russian novels center considerably around the samovar, as though it were a hearth. . . . For that matter, if you're one of the lucky people with a fireplace, have a fire when you're alone of an evening, as well as when you have guests. If you like to lounge with your feet up, have a soft chair with a hassock. And if you think there's nothing more satisfying than a chaise longue with an afghan at its foot when you have a cold (or when you haven't), then get yourself one.

The kind of pampering I am talking about also involves having bedroom curtains thick enough to keep out the morning light if you like to sleep of a Sunday morning (there's something called milium, a kind of silvery-looking blackout material that you can buy in a department store to line draperies, if yours aren't lined). It means having sheets with purple chrysanthemums or yellow daisies on them, instead of having hospital white. For true luxury in a bedroom, nothing can match a low, solid, roomy table as a bedside table, one that is just the height of your bed, runs parallel to it, and is about forty inches long. It should hold a tall lamp, a telephone (why is it that in movies people just reach out of bed and pick up the telephone, but in real life most people have to stumble across a room in the dark to get to it?), and a clock-radio. It will have room for books, and it should have a box of cleaning tissues, and a tall mug that holds an emery board or two, pencils, and an extra pair of glasses (if you wear glasses) for viewing television. The reasonable place for a television set is where you can see it from bed. And wastebaskets. Wastebaskets don't sound like much of a princess-with-a-pea kind of luxury, but they are—if you don't have one in every room, try it, and you'll see how it eases life.

Pleasures like these are both sensory and aesthetic, so the more the better. It is a greater pleasure to look out of sparkling clean windows than out of dirty windows, for instance (but no pleasure at all to clean them, so don't do it yourself; in New York it costs me six dollars for a window cleaner to clean bedroom and living room windows, five big windows in all, and a great investment at $1.20 per window). It is also a luxury to close out noise (which is probably why expensive restaurants are often referred to as "quietly elegant"), so try to afford carpeting that absorbs noise. If you can afford a beautiful rug or rugs, so much the better. If you enjoy music, have good hi-fi equipment or your ear won't be happy with what it hears when you have private concerts. Even if you don't care anything about music, have good equipment anyway if it suits the kind of entertaining you do.

Having a bathroom to yourself is a luxury only the live-aloner or the very rich can have, and it's worth making the most of. You have all that cabinet space for your cosmetics and so on—which is a good reason for seeing that they stay inside the cabinet and not scattered around, and on the windowsill, since a bathroom ought to be as aesthetically pleasing as any other room. If you like Dufy seaside prints or prints of rosy Rubens ladies emerging from the bath, have them on the walls. Hang up a big mirror in a wide frame if you like mirrors. Have the biggest, fluffiest bath towel in the world to wrap yourself in after a shower or bath, and have a beautiful shower curtain (even if you have to make it yourself) and a rug to keep your feet off the cold floor, and a scale to keep track of your weight. If you have a counter top, convenient things to keep on it are a box of dusting powder, with a brilliant-colored puff, a table-top wastebasket, a bottle of cologne, and a jar (maybe Japanese), that holds combs; also a box, such as one of those gilded Renaissance boxes, is perfect for holding whatever kinds of hair clips or pins you use. Besides having a bright light in the bathroom (and a button light for a faint glow at night), a nice thing to have is a shaded wall lamp that sheds a soft light that makes your guests feel more attractive than they do when they glimpse themselves in your cabinet mirror under stark bright light. Stark light doesn't do much for your own morale either, so use it only when you need it.

Whatever you do with your apartment, be relaxed about doing it. The fact that it will mirror your taste alone (you can't for instance blame those curtains or that cushion on a housemate) is often enough to petrify a live-aloner, like a rabbit frozen before the fox. After all, to do *anything,* to make a single decision, is to commit yourself. I know an otherwise self-assured public relations assistant who doesn't dare choose a fabric or a piece of furniture or decide on a rug, for fear she'll reveal she has no taste, no style, no imagination. Instead, she embarrassedly prefers to meet her dinner dates in the lobby of her apartment building. And she never dares invite a man in for coffee and cognac after dinner.

I know a secretary who ordered a chest of drawers and then left it in its packing case for two months while she went through agonies of anxiety over just where it would look right . . . or perhaps she should send it back? I know a smart young woman who is so blocked by her fear of what her decorating attempts might reveal that she lives in a furnished apartment that's as uninspiring as a dead fish—but at least, she feels, nobody can say it's a fish *she* created. It's also costing her a pretty penny to live this comfortless way, since rather than come home to her dreary furnished apartment she stays out spending money in department stores and restaurants. If you're one of the petrified, it might help you loosen up if you realize that *doing nothing* is just as revealing as doing *something*. Living luxuriously as an Egyptian queen tells something about you, but so does living like an underprivileged Eliza Doolittle.

You might just as well, therefore, go ahead and be more comfortable at least, without trying to be a perfectionist about it. You can start out by realizing that you'll have initial grace and comfort if you have an oasis of a good-looking chair and a lamp you can read by. Beyond that, you might add a soft couch if you like soft couches or a hard one if you like hard. Have three or four chairs you can draw up when you have guests and a scattering of three or four low tables big enough to hold an ash tray, a drink and a few other things, and perhaps a lamp. A big coffee table is wonderful, the bigger the better, even as big as a cut-down round old dining-room table—big enough, anyway, to hold plates of hors d'oeuvres, magazines, highball glasses, some bottles. You can accumulate things slowly, but the point is to *start* . . . and then to keep an eye out for furnishings and eye-attracting effects that please you in shops, antique stores, decorating books, furniture stores. Gradually the room will take shape, but well before it's finished (if ever) it will be a place you'll enjoy living in. And it will certainly be a lot better than what you had.

Then there is live-alone housekeeping which is quite a different story from housekeeping when you live with other people. Live-alone housekeeping is simpler, of course, than the other kind, since the only ring in the bathtub is yours and the only magazines and clothes strewn around to be picked up are strewn around by you. There is also no one to complain about any disarray—a fact that can be not only a blessing but a danger. I am thinking of one live-aloner whose apartment usually gives the impression of being waist deep in last Sunday's *Times*. Getting to a chair is like hacking one's way through an Amazonian rain forest. This situation is seldom appreciated by visitors, and it really doesn't do much for the apartment owner's temper either.

One secret to having a fresh-looking apartment is to see that what needs to be polished and gleaming is kept polished and gleaming. Assuming you don't have help, part-time or otherwise, if you enjoy polishing brass and the bottoms of copper-bottomed pots, then have plenty of them. But if you hate polishing then don't have copper-bottomed pots unless you hide them in the kitchen cabinet; as for brass and so on, lacquer it so it stays bright without polishing or replace it with glazed pottery that you can simply wash.

A good rule is to attack immediately any unaesthetic look that crops up overnight, such as a tear in a lampshade or a crooked venetian blind. If you don't, it will be a subliminal irritation several times an evening, while you promise yourself *I must do something about that* . . . and then suddenly it's too late because you have unexpected guests or someone invites you to dinner and comes to pick you up, and there he is—standing in your living room beside a torn lampshade or dingy draperies.

An apartment with empty closets is a thousand times easier to take care of than one where you're in danger of concussion every time you open a closet door. So the emptier your closets, the better. Closets and cabinets that are as empty as a Sahara landscape would be ideal, but at least yours should be empty of everything you accumulated in a bigger house, a former marriage, or an earlier apartment that may have been Mexican in motif whereas your mood (and present furniture investment) may now be Chinese. Get rid of duplicates of appliances, extra flashlights and thermos bottles, half-filled cans of paint, and a thousand other things you probably won't ever use. It may give you a twinge to part with something like a handmade rug you lugged all the way from Venezuela or Nevada (it gave me one), but don't let that stop you. Once you've cleared everything out, you'll revel in those beautifully empty closets and cabinets where you can actually *find things*. And your apartment will have a lovely feeling of spaciousness.

Household repairs are another story, usually a grimmer one. Having no man in the house is a situation that can cost a pretty penny and lots of aggravation when it comes to fixing a broken toaster, a leaky faucet, an eccentric light switch. Getting a plumber, electrician, or handyman to come and fix anything is as likely as finding gold nuggets in the street. Right here is where a live-aloner has to avoid falling into the trap of the tempting helpless-without-a-man syndrome. "I'm such an idiot when it comes to appliances," a widow friend of mine says winningly, helplessly, to an electrician she hopes will find time to fix her vacuum cleaner. But this kind of plea only sends the bill up a few dollars. Misanthropic as it sounds, there are indeed people who take advantage of you if they get the impression that you're a helpless and ignorant female who thinks electricity is something that works with a kite and lightning. You'll get better results, better workmanship, better prices by being as knowledgeable as possible, woman alone or not. And pleading is beneath your dignity.

If you're even remotely handy, the ideal way to deal with household repairs is to do them yourself. It's an exhilarating surprise when you discover there is no magic trick to fixing a leaky faucet, wiring a plug, or repairing a lamp switch. At Goucher College, a course for girls called "Nuts and Bolts" is arousing a lot of enthusiasm, so you can see which way the wind is blowing. The course teaches how to fix dead lamps, vacuum cleaners, television sets, toasters, radios, and it includes simple repairs and how to cope with irritating things like doors that stick, broken plaster, and those dozens of other things that a woman can really do herself. You can learn a number of these same things in many suburban adult education courses too—in New York they're called "Leisure Courses for Adults," though why fixing a leaky faucet comes under the heading of "leisure" is more than a little puzzling. Or you can learn how to do at least some home repairs from fix-it books. Adult books—even those for amateurs—are a little intimidating at first, but fix-it books for twelve-year-olds are ideal, and if you're lucky your library has one or two. You save all kinds of money and the frustration of dealing with repair men who can come only between three and five when you're going to be home only between six and eight.

Once you start repairing things on your own, it's a short step to installing all kinds of little conveniences no electrician would bother installing for you anyway. The directions come with almost anything you buy at the hardware store, and it's very gratifying when you discover that in less than fifteen minutes you can clamp a tiny switch onto a bedside lamp cord, so it's within inches of your hand, and you never have to reach up to turn out the light. You can install dimmers to dim or brighten your living room lamps, and "tap" light switches that also glow in the dark, and you can install front-door chimes if you like chimes.

What with one thing and another, you can provide yourself with most if not all the conveniences of the presidential suite at the New York Hilton.

CHAPTER 7

Entertaining

If plenty of friends reasonably often telephone you and invite you to dinners and parties, it is invariably true that you in turn have been inviting *them*. But if, as happens to most live-aloners, almost as though it were an occupational hazard, you find yourself with a lost *Where-is-everybody?* feeling, you are probably not doing your share of entertaining. Or perhaps you are doing none at all?

Everybody, of course, is right there. But they are not going to keep on entertaining you (or even start to) unless you entertain them, too. Besides, when you meet one person or another you'd like for a friend, the best way to ripen that relationship is to entertain her (or him). Friends, like carrots and certain flowers, have to be cultivated—and what better way to cultivate them than to entertain them?

I am not suggesting you shower guests with caviar or feed them elaborate canapés with a truffle in the middle. A reasonable range of entertaining might extend from inviting one person to share a simple supper and an evening of conversation, to having six people in for chili and beer, or eight for dinner, or a couple of dozen for a buffet, or for whatever you can afford. You can do some of these things or you can do all of them, or just one that pleases you. The meat and drink of life is socializing . . . and the purpose, after all, is warmth and friendship, knowing people with whom you can share confidences and pleasures. An hour of companionship over a cup of tea can be worth more than all the expensive caviar in Iran.

When it comes right down to it, most of the memorable or heartwarming evenings in a person's life are involved with people getting together and enjoying food and drink. Naturally, you want to entertain in such a way that your guests will identify those delightful times with you. It won't hurt. Neither will it hurt when they begin asking you back, inviting you to meet their friends. And so, via a little persistent entertaining, you can't help but develop a satisfying social life.

When I say persistent, I mean just that. You might, for instance, invite fourteen people to a buffet supper, and in return maybe one person will invite you back the following month. The fact is that an amazing number of likable people won't ask you back at first because *they* have never got into the habit of entertaining; they don't know how easy and friendly entertaining can be. But they might well pick up the habit from you. If they don't, and you like them anyway, keep on inviting them. You are not out to reform the social world but to enjoy it.

Entertaining has all kinds of advantages for the live-aloner. It is curious but true that when people have been in your home, they view you differently. Their attitude changes. You gain some sort of background, a setting they can see. It rounds you out, in their eye. You can generally bank on it that entertaining someone in your home will change a ships-that-pass-in-the-night acquaintance-ship into something more stable. This is particularly important when you live alone; you haven't, after all, the stability of being part of a family or a couple. You are not *part* of anything; you're the whole works, somebody establishing her own identity, her own setting. So when you invite people and entertain them, they can fill in the hazy part of their image of you—you take shape, you make an imprint. How impressive after all would Heathcliff be without our seeing him against the background of Wuthering Heights? . . . And Cathy, how would she have struck us if we'd only met her on Main Street?

You don't need a fancy, big apartment for entertaining—the idea isn't to overpower people (you're not running for public office, after all) but to make your guests feel relaxed and happy, to have *friends*. The apology "My apartment is too small for a party" is laughable in the 1970s. Even if you have one room and a kitchenette-in-the-wall, you can offer a friend a drink, or a couple of friends a candlelit supper, or even have a group of people in for a party. A friend of mine who had a one-room apartment with a sleeping alcove got her carpentry-minded brother to wall off the alcove; the "wall" was merely two rows of floor to ceiling poles with wood panels that could slide between them. If you have a one-room apartment and you don't mind a convertible couch for a bed, you can have that much more alcove space for entertaining. No room has ever been big enough for a party, anyway, not even the White House or Blair House. And it is a safe bet that when Louis XIV gave parties at Versailles, the place was too small.

Yet some live-aloners give the best, most enjoyable parties in small quarters, where the hostess can barely furnish a half-dozen chairs. I know one popular live-aloner who creates a bar by setting up a card table in her bedroom doorway. I know another who has no bedroom, but she does own a set of iron table legs, and on them she places the two extra leaves from an old dining-room table, thereby creating a sideboard buffet which she loads with delicious homemade bread, a baked ham, mustard pickles and cole slaw . . . and her guests always have a wonderful time. The point here is not ever to be embarrassed or ashamed about the smallness of your apartment if it's all your budget can afford. I remember once, when I was in Rome to do a magazine story, I met a snobbish, fading celebrity who disdainfully mentioned a young publisher's assistant, telling me, "She has a pocket-sized apartment . . . so tiny that at her last party somebody spilled spaghetti in Marcello Mastroianni's lap." I remember gasping with envy of the young assistant with that pocket-sized apartment. The fact is, of course, that no matter how cramped the quarters, if there are a few congenial people to share some conversation and laughter, your party is a success, whereas you can be bored blue in the handsomest apartment and a servant at your elbow every second with fancy canapés.

If you're apprehensive about entertaining because of the awful thought: *What if something goes wrong?* it is easiest to accept the fact that something probably will. What of it? The most unforgettable parties are those during which something did go wrong. I remember once going to a party in Hopewell Junction, New York, a party that started out stiffly with a dozen strangers on a back patio—at least they were strangers until the wooden table that held a gigantic bowl of rum punch suddenly collapsed. But who could stay strangers then, with some people mopping, some picking up glass, several others offering to drive to the liquor store, and everybody helping? One of the guests later remarked to me that it was the best party he'd ever been to.

Sometimes what goes wrong will go wrong among the guests, of course. Still, in John O'Hara's *Appointment in Samarra,* for instance, there wouldn't even have been any story if Julian English hadn't thrown a highball in someone's face. It can happen at a private party (yours) as well as at an O'Hara country club. Of course you should mingle your guests sensibly enough for relative harmony. But it is silly to worry that you might not have a perfectly harmonious party with everybody enchanted by everybody else, particularly since all that harmony can get pretty boring anyway. An English couple, who recently wrote a book on astrology, even go so far as to say that when they want to give a party they decide what emotions would suit their mood—some rousing hostility to stimulate them, or perhaps a calm, friendly evening? Then they cast a few friends' horoscopes and invite the ones who'll produce the effect they want. If you're reasonably acute, you won't have to cast horoscopes to know who'll mix or clash. But while a little clashing can enliven a party, it is advisable not to go too far, as did one unfortunate live-aloner who invited me to a supper for eight, and as I arrived the door flew open and out stormed an enraged-looking couple. My hostess explained tearfully, as she took my coat, that over the drinks and appetizers this angry couple had had a violent divergence of political opinion with another guest. Their rage had carried them away—right out the door. Stimulation is fine, but your aim, after all, is to invite people for an enjoyable evening, which is hardly what you'd be likely to get if you invited, say, William Buckley and Gore Vidal to the same party.

When it comes to entertaining, a live-aloner holds some very good cards. When you live alone you have the advantage of cultivating people because you find them witty, aware, interesting, amusing—and not because they come in married pairs. You can cultivate more live-aloners than ever before, since there are more people living alone these days. A few years ago, they would have been considered lame ducks (as you might have been, too). But since lame ducks have taken to piloting their own planes or joining Nader's Raiders, they are more likely to be running the show than watching it, and almost anything they have to say is worth listening to. Naturally, when you invite such friends, your party is going to be a lot more interesting than the average suburban or city party with its sets of married couples.

Odd numbers are in, and the Noah's Ark method of inviting isn't important any longer—women come without men, men without women, and a party of five, seven, or nine is as acceptable as an even-numbered party. And whoever your guests are, they're *your* choice: You are not, blessedly, obliged to entertain a housemate's old college chums or a roommate's girl friends, or a married partner's business associates.

If you are timorous about inviting people because you're afraid they'll turn you down, you had better get over it as quickly as possible or you'll be living in solitary confinement. Most people are pleased and flattered to be invited to a party. And they'll come. Of course a few will turn you down, but that fact shouldn't be so devastating that you feel it's equivalent to being sent to the gallows. You can live with it.

The more you can convince yourself to be casual about inviting people, the easier you'll find it is to pick up the telephone and ask people in. And we do mean *telephone*. Practically everybody these days invites guests by telephone, and it's less nerve-wracking than writing notes, because you get an answer immediately, instead of having to wait and wonder who's coming and who isn't. If you're the nervous type, and the mails being what they are, you can become quite paranoid, what with waiting for answers. So, telephone. And when you do telephone, of course be sure to call people at home and not at their office, and be sure to invite them personally.

If you're nervous about inviting people to parties, you'll feel more courageous if you have an excuse for giving one. A *reason* for inviting them. It won't really matter what the reason is: Invite people in to celebrate a promotion, or invite them to celebrate your new apartment, or having paid off your fur coat or having got a doctorate. A lighthearted friend of mine once telephoned me the first week in May with the excuse that "Suddenly it's spring, and I'm giving a May wine party to celebrate it," and so she did, with a strawberry in each glass of springlike May wine (and with non-strawberry highballs, too), and sandwiches. It was such a success that she has turned it into an annual party, and she'll call up people and say simply, "I'm having my May Wine party on Saturday afternoon," and people look forward to it every year.

Giving a party *for someone* is an ideal excuse. Have a party for your cousin Myra who is in town from St. Paul for a few weeks, have a party for Charles J. who has been transferred back from the coast, have a party for your friend Genevieve B. who is just back from Alaska. What with people going and coming, you'll have plenty of excuses to give parties for them. And don't forget their accomplishments, which ought to be celebrated. "Joanna W. has illustrated a children's book, and it's just out and I'm having a buffet party for her" is in this category. Don't wait for them to climb Mount Everest.

Giving a party for another person also relieves you of a lot of figuring out whom to invite, because you ask your honored guest for a half-dozen names of her (or his) friends they'd like to have you ask. That of course also gives you the opportunity to meet a few new people. And for some peculiar reason, it is much easier to call up those perfect strangers and say, "I'm so-and-so, and I'm having a party for Myra N. and would love to have you come." It is rather on the same principle as those executives who are nervous wrecks if they have to go job-hunting for themselves, but who can with perfect aplomb sell other executives into jobs.

Giving a party for somebody also makes them love you dearly, and sooner or later, when you go to Yugoslavia or someplace, when you return *they* might even give a party for *you*. So, in a way, it's a social investment.

Figuring out whom to invite to a party is always rather like a word game, putting down names and then taking them out; fitting and refitting, juggling and rejuggling. And what names do you start with? Instead of going through your address book, you might, as I do, have a "People" folder. Whenever I meet someone I like, I jot down their name and address and drop it into my "People" folder, which also contains the names of my personal friends. When I want to invite a few people for dinner, or give a party, there are all the names—this editor and his girl; that new widow of a travel agent (met at another party); the twenty-eight-year-old women's lib writer met last week; the bachelor who used to live next door. There's that interesting couple I met at a relative's New Year's eggnog party in Mamaroneck, another couple met in Martinique, a young psychiatrist who lives in my building. The whole idea of a folder is simply because it's so much easier to remember the people you meet here and there, and really like; otherwise they just might slip your mind.

So, having made up your list, ask them. *Ask them*. Even if it feels like going over Niagara Falls in a barrel, ask them. You will get pleased acceptances from almost everybody, and a couple of regretful replies from others who have previous appointments, or who say they have. When a person can't come, don't waste time analyzing why not, or you'll decide nobody likes you. Just put their names aside, and maybe give them one more chance, later on, at another party. If they're busy again, with a limp explanation, drop the slip gently in the wastebasket. One thing that's sure death for a party is having a guest who really doesn't want to come, so don't ever press people.

Invite, if you can, one or two heart-steadying good friends, since they're solid security, rather like the trunk of the tree, with the other guests as branches. I generally ask a good friend or two to come a half-hour earlier than the other guests, for moral support and to "break in the room"—to give it a feeling of the party having started, when the next guests arrive.

When you do invite people, you ought to at least attempt to invite them two weeks ahead of time, or, in a pinch, a week ahead. Otherwise of course they may have already made other dates, and you'll have to go back to revamping your list. Once everyone *has* accepted, you can start worrying that some of them might forget. If the day before the party you are nervously tempted to call everybody back, to remind them of the date and time, don't be embarrassed about it—call them. I do. Why bother worrying?

But what if you'd suddenly like to invite people in for . . . *tomorrow night?* A last-minute inspiration? Perhaps your weekend plans have been called off and you're suddenly free, restless, and stricken with a case of loneliness . . . and you think it would be a wonderful idea to ask a handful of people in to dinner. Or else you're the last-minute type who hates to make plans way in advance (and in your book "way in advance" means three days). Or you may simply always be too nervous about inviting people, but given to sudden longings for a gregarious evening: One of the bravest women I know (last year she went down the Colorado Rapids in a canoe, alone) becomes jittery at the idea of inviting a few people in for dinner weeks in advance—but then suddenly she yearns to ask them for day after tomorrow and doesn't know how. She usually is so afraid she'll offend friends by last-minute invitations, that she ends up calling nobody at all.

Inviting people at the last minute takes a bit of *élan*. But you can learn it. I know one woman who is a late-planner, and a champion at it. When she telephones you on Thursday and asks you to dinner on Friday, you find yourself going. How does she do it? She sounds so impulsive and spontaneous that before you know it, you are caught up into thinking she has just come up with a stupendous, remarkable, delightful inspiration—dinner at her house tomorrow night! She never, for one thing, goes on the assumption that you're available, that you have nothing to do, and she always has some special reason (no matter how miniscule) for the party being a last-minute affair. "I've just learned how to make *couscous*," she will tell you exuberantly, "—and you've *got* to come! I know it's spur-of-the-moment, but are you possibly free? Linda X. and the Walters brothers are coming, too, I just talked to them." This lets her guest know that she's not a "fill-in" asked at the last minute because she might be available; it is always good to mention that you "just talked to" somebody or other who will be coming. And convey that it's all such a sudden inspiration, and fun. It's also a good idea to ask a close friend or two first (like Linda X. and the Walters brothers)—the kind of friends who have no qualms about accepting last-minute invitations if they're free; this gives you a chance to mention that they're coming, too. You are using them, quite bluntly, as pride-saving "bait."

I'm going to persist a little here, on the subject of saving an invitee's pride when you telephone a last-minute invitation. After all, you're not out to bag guests with a butterfly net, but with taste and tact. Use both, copiously. For instance, "Are you possibly going to be in town on Monday? . . . I know you're always off on those long ski weekends" lets your invitee know you're perfectly aware she's not wasting away with loneliness by the telephone, waiting for dinner invitations. If you have to, lie a little. "You're always so busy, but you remember so-and-so? . . . Well, he just came in from California, and I'm asking him and a couple of other people to dinner; he's dying to see you, and can you possibly come, too?" may be stretching the truth about so-and-so's feelings, and maybe so-and-so has been in town from California for a week already, but what of it?

Almost anything you say along these lines gives people an easy way to say they'd love to come, with no pride hurt. Even the busiest, most popular people in the world have free evenings or sometimes lonely ones, and they welcome an occasional last-minute invitation, but they want to feel that you *know* they're popular and busy. So make them feel it. They will practically fall into the telephone saying Yes, if you make it intimate and fun with "What are you doing for dinner tomorrow night? . . . I haven't seen you for ages, and I'm asking a couple of other people in . . . Can you come?" Whereas if you invite them with an unvarnished "Can you come to dinner tomorrow night?" they'll feel a cold draft down the back of their neck, and may save their pride by telling you they're booked solid for the next six months.

If you're new to a city or town you may know hardly anyone, and you have the special problem of finding anyone at all to invite. You can't knit a woolen sweater without wool. A live-aloner in this situation will have to do a little casting around to meet new friends (we go into the "how to" of meeting them in the next chapter). But if you've moved to the city from nearby suburbs or country, you probably do have some favorite suburban or country friends you can draw on. If you think they wouldn't like to come all the way into town for a party, ask them anyway. You'll be surprised how many will be delighted to make a two-hour drive from Massachusetts to New York City, or from Batavia, Illinois, to Chicago, or into Nashville or Topeka to get to your simple buffet party.

Why? Perhaps socializing with people they truly like makes it worth it to them. Or maybe they find such a distraction a breath of relief, a break in routine. Maybe they just want to get away from their children. Or enjoy driving. Or maybe it comes under the heading of adventure . . . who knows? But anyway, they come.

If you live in the suburbs, you may have to look harder if you're going to collect a satisfying circle of friends to invite, but you can find them: A young biochemist friend of mine who works in a hospital laboratory in suburban Riverdale invited me to one of the most enjoyable parties I can remember: the guests were a man who taught French at a nearby private school, a woman who was a green-thumb florist who ran a small greenhouse business from her own back yard, a woman psychiatrist, a Swiss divorcée who worked in the local women's sports shop, and two male biochemists.

A relative you've always met only at big family Thanksgiving dinners can even be uncovered as a gem, if you take the risk and invite him (or her). Oddly, when you cut a relative out of the herd you can often—for the first time—meet the whole person. It happened inadvertently to a friend of mine, an English girl of about twenty-six, who on the day of giving her first party to new friends in New York, received a telephone call from an elderly great-aunt who had just arrived on a visit from South Africa. Hospitality demanded that Great-Aunt Esmé be invited, and she was, despite the hostess's qualms. Aunt Esmé, though, turned out to be the star of the party, what with her tales of South Africa. So you never can tell. Mixing people of different ages and interests is a good idea anyway—it makes for a more dynamic party.

Perhaps the best rule in inviting people is to invite the people you genuinely like; when you do, almost all of them will gladly accept. This is possibly because genuine liking seems to communicate itself. I have one friend who is young and has a small salary, but she writes newspaper feature stories, so she gets to meet any number of well-known people whom she has to interview. Those she honestly likes she invites to an occasional Sunday brunch party at her rented suburban home on Long Island. Most of these well-known people come, usually by train, and she picks them up at the station in her rattly old 1963 Chevvy. But I once met a lady who courts celebrities out of snobbishness, and she can't understand why they turn down her engraved invitations.

Worrying about food and how to serve the lavish best, and if your guests will all admire or love you for it, has frightened more than one live-aloner into being a social dropout. Sad and unnecessary. You really don't have to be the mother, pressing food on everyone. And neither should you expect to be judged as though you were crossing swords with Craig Claiborne or James Beard. If what you give your guests is reasonably tasty, they're bound to feel expansive and friendly. Anxiety is only a waste of energy. . . . I know one otherwise confident young art assistant at an ad agency, who, when she moved into her first live-alone apartment last year and began inviting friends to dinner, always served *two* desserts, in case her guests might not like one of them. Her anxiety was so close to the nail-biting stage that it didn't make for a very festive atmosphere. But by her fourth small dinner she began to relax; these days when she has people to dinner she serves a simple dessert like a peeled orange sprinkled with coconut, or a wedge of cheese with crackers. Her guests have a better time, mainly because of her more insouciant attitude.

As for what live-alone entertaining costs, a fine piece of luck is that when a woman lives alone, friends don't expect her to entertain elaborately and expensively. In fact, even the rich and social entertain informally these days. If we want to go way back, maybe Eleanor Roosevelt started the whole informality trend when, back in the 1930s, she entertained the King and Queen of England at a hotdogs-and-cokes picnic. Now sophisticated political folk in New York or Washington, D.C. frequently hire a hotdog wagon for a party, complete with umbrella, hotdogs, mustard, rolls, and a man to serve it all. At a recent dinner for charity, socialites and other folk like the British Ambassador to the United Nations dined at the Automat on roast beef and were given a dollar in change to buy their own desserts (they were supposed to return the money if they were on a diet). And a few years ago I happened to be one of several magazine editors invited by Charlotte Ford to a Lyndon Johnson party given at the Fords', at Bridgehampton, and what I remember most was socialites and celebrities and everyone else ecstatically devouring buttered sweet corn, spare ribs, and Texas "soul food." We ate bread in hunks and we ate chicken off paper plates, and we ate everything with our fingers, and everybody loved it. What with hardly anybody entertaining fancily any more, you can safely offer your guests the simplest of pleasures.

If you're new to living alone, it's a good idea to start small. By small, I mean perhaps having a friend or two in for supper . . . maybe after a Saturday afternoon movie. It's an easy way to get the "feel" of entertaining, and of finding out what accoutrements you're lacking, such as decent-looking salt and pepper shakers or a coffeepot that doesn't make you blush at its battered past. When you finally don't cringe at the basics you're using, you're off to a good start. You'll also be able to see how to expand for larger groups. It is much the same principle as in the story of that mythological hero who started out by lifting a baby calf every day so that as it grew up he was eventually able to lift the whole ox. Not that you should ever give up entertaining small: One of the pure pleasures of living alone is the intimacy and charm of entertaining small. A table by a window, at 7:00 o'clock of a summer's evening, with a couple of friends, and a supper of cold sliced meat, hot rolls, salad, and iced tea isn't that much trouble; but it makes an evening worth looking back on. The best of friendships often stem from such easy evenings. In winter, when it gets dark early, entertaining "small" is even cozier than fleece-lined slippers.

When you live alone, you have the advantage of impulse inviting—at the last minute impulsively asking a couple of friends in for supper, which is something you can't very well do when you live with other people or even with one other person. A nice thing about extending an impulsive invitation is that you don't have to live up to anything fancy, since the whole thing is extemporaneous. Any number of delicious things come in cans—meats, soups, fish, and so on—as anybody over the age of three knows, and you might as well keep a few on your kitchen shelf. Then there are all those pastas and noodle combinations that come in packages, and any number of things you can keep in a freezer . . . and half-bottles of wine you can buy for 89¢ or a dollar, and whole bottles of very good wines you can buy for two dollars. With such supplies you can come up with any number of delicious little suppers: for instance a glass of dry red wine, Noodles Romanoff with sour cream cheese sauce (all from a package), and a broiled lamb chop, followed by coffee. You can spend a half hour with almost any good cookbook and come up with ideas for a dozen simple but delectable suppers. Almost anything you make, your friends will love you for anyway. A Danish friend of mine who is all of twenty-four, yet is already an assistant art director on a magazine, has developed the habit of asking a couple of friends for supper at least twice a month. She gives them first a tiny glass of aquavit that would melt a glacier. Then, at the table, which is a card table covered with a maroon felt cloth, she ladles out steaming lentil soup (with a dash of sherry) and serves it with a plate of sausages and rye bread. No dessert. You eat by candlelight and you finish with easy talk over a cup of tea. Most people can't wait to be invited to this Scandinavian feast.

Once you get into the swing of entertaining, you can even become addicted to it. But, as I implied earlier, as with learning to swim, it makes sense not to fling yourself into too deep water or you risk being panicked away from it for good. So unless you're an old hand at entertaining, you might graduate from "small" entertaining to the next simplest kind, which is the Sunday brunch.

Don't be surprised if when you say to people, "Can you come for brunch at one o'clock on Sunday" they respond with such pleased surprise that you'd think you'd just dropped a golden apple in their lap. Sunday brunch is one of those delightful, homey social pleasures that people somehow forget about. But they love to be reminded. This is particularly true of most of the single men and women friends a live-aloner has more of than anybody else. Any number of them usually neglect to make plans beyond buying the Sunday papers, so a congenial Sunday brunch in the offing will be a minor form of paradise. This puts you, as the hostess, way ahead, since practically anything you give them beyond a fragrant cup of hot coffee will taste delicious. Besides, they (and you) needn't worry about Monday morning, since this is an afternoon occasion. Guests at a brunch are more relaxed, too, since there's nothing to live up to; nobody ever feels he has to be violently social or vivacious on a Sunday afternoon, which is a great relief. One man, a city planner who spends an exhausting week, claims the best part of any Sunday brunch is when in the late afternoon "conversation drifts away and it all gets a little boring and peaceful."

A comfortable number of people to ask to brunch is from six to ten. If you don't know the procedure, it's simple enough: You ask your guests for noon or 1:00 o'clock, and give them an hour or so to drink their Bloody Marys or Screwdrivers. If you like a sitting-around-a-table atmosphere (I do) and if you have a table big enough, have everybody sit down together to eat. Or they can perch on hassocks and eat off coffee tables or end tables, if that suits you better.

Since brunch is really a hearty breakfast, and since almost anybody can cook breakfast, there's no point in telling you how. The simplest Sunday brunch, and one that everyone seems to love is an omelet with sausages or thick-sliced ham, hot rolls with strawberry jam and butter, and pots of fresh coffee. Just give your guests plenty of all this and they'll be in heaven. Get the rolls from a bakery, and buy an already cooked ham in the supermarket and heat it. Variations are infinite. You might want to skip the jam and end the meal with something sweet—a coffee cake is good.

Serve whatever suits you, whatever you find easiest to make: bacon and waffles with honey, or maybe blueberry pancakes (blueberries out of a can), or apple pancakes with crisp bacon. If you're crazy about French toast and think you make it particularly well, make it. If you're a poor hand at cookery, you can buy packaged everything almost, from bake-and-serve croissants to pancake mixes, to biscuits, rolls, and so on.

From a timorous beginning, you might wind up serving brunches with considerable style. An executive secretary who, when I first knew her, had never cooked, nervously started out serving English muffins, bacon, and coffee. But within months she graduated to hot homemade biscuits and Philadelphia scrapple. Nowadays she is so full of confidence that when she has people in for brunch she is liable to serve them the kind of fare you read about in novels about English manor house living—kidneys and bacon, and so on, all from covered dishes on a sideboard that is really a bookcase shelf she clears for the occasion; the guests then carry their plates to her big table, also just as in those British country houseparty stories she likes. Whatever she gives her guests, though, they gobble it up. She has no dining room (what live-aloner has?) and the table takes up two-thirds of the living room when the leaves are in, and they are in at least one Sunday a month. That's a lot of brunches, but it is the only kind of entertaining she does—though it is not the only way she is entertained, since her guests respond by asking her to everything from movies to dinners to the theater.

Happily, brunch is also the least expensive kind of entertaining you can do. If your budget is small, you can cut down in a dozen ways, instead of letting costs discourage you. A free-lance jewelry designer I know, sometimes has an off-season and her finances get low; when this happens she gives a brunch anyway, but simply switches from serving eggs to serving pancakes, since you can make forty-eight good-sized pancakes with only four eggs, as any good cookbook will tell you. My friend serves hers with warmed honey, cinnamon, and crisp bacon. You can also make simple and delicious eggless griddle cakes, which most cookbooks do *not* tell you, and if you don't know how, the how of it is to sift together 3 cups of flour, 1½ tablespoons of baking powder, 1 teaspoon of salt. Then stir in two cups of milk and then 2 tablespoons of oil or margarine. Drop by spoonfuls on a hot griddle or into a frying pan, just as you would any other pancakes. You'll have plenty of pancakes—about thirty—with this quantity. They taste just as good as other pancakes, though naturally they're not as nourishing. However, your friends haven't come to brunch for bodily nourishment anyway, but for social nourishment.

The budgetary corners you can cut are plentiful and include things like serving bread because it is less expensive than rolls, stretching eggs by making French toast, making your own rolls instead of buying mixes, or packaged or baked rolls. The vodka you buy for the Bloody Marys and Screwdrivers can be the least expensive possible; vodka is vodka, despite the status labels. Some vodka is a higher proof than others—that is, it has a slightly higher percentage of alcohol—but nobody really cares which it is, at least nobody I've ever met. One vodka tastes like another, and in any case no connoisseur on earth could tell the difference once it's in a Bloody Mary or a Screwdriver.

In a financial pinch, or just for the satisfaction of it, you might even want to make your own hot biscuits, as I occasionally do. The simplest recipe I know takes about two minutes. You sift together 4 cups of flour and 8 teaspoons of baking powder and 2 teaspoons of salt. Then work 4 tablespoons of oil or margarine into the mixture with your fingertips. Then gradually mix in 2 cups of water or milk. That's it. Drop by spoonfuls onto a greased pan, one inch apart, or else drop in muffin pan, filling each little cup about two thirds full. Bake your biscuits in a 450°F oven for 10 to 15 minutes. They're delicious. If you're going to do this often, keep your muffin pan, flour, salt, and baking powder in one convenient corner of the kitchen cabinet.

And there's the egg, of course, which gives you any number of opportunities to be simple or exotic, what with Eggs Benedict, curried eggs, scrambled eggs or perhaps eggs topped with sour cream and red caviar, and all those other kinds of eggs. There are about ten cookbooks on eggs alone, including one telling you what to do when you're stuck with leftover whites or yolks, so you shouldn't have any trouble. You probably have one kind of egg dish you make best and are happy with. But if you haven't, a good one is the sensational French omelet that helped make Rudolph Stanish become known as the Omelet King. Mr. Stanish has since retired, but the omelets he cooked were good enough to have international society send to New York for Mr. Stanish when they were giving a breakfast in Scotland or Paris or elsewhere in Europe, so you can see that he served up a mean omelet. In the line of editorial duties when I was on a magazine, I once attended a business lunch where I ate three of Mr. Stanish's omelets, watched him at work for an hour while he performed his egg magic, and eventually came away with instructions he was good enough to give me. If you want to try this omelet and make it yours, here it is: For 5 omelets, break 12 eggs into a large bowl. Combine 3 tablespoons of water, ½ teaspoon salt, and ¼ teaspoon Tabasco; then add them to the eggs. Beat the mixture with an eggbeater until blended but not frothy. Melt a tablespoon of butter in the pan, and when the pan is hot enough—it's hot enough when a drop of water sizzles on it—add one-fifth of the egg mixture. Then cook it the classic way an omelet should be cooked—that is, hold the pan handle in your left hand with the palm down, moving the pan in a back-and-forth motion. Your right hand holds the fork and moves in a circular motion. About seven circular motions or so (it takes me about twenty, but you may like a very soft omelet) and the omelet is ready to be turned out. All you do then is to reverse the position of your left hand, placing it so that you're holding the handle of the pan with your palm upward. Now you simply tip the pan and, with a gentle prod of the fork, roll the omelet out onto a warm dish. Mr. Stanish didn't have to prod, but almost everyone else will, at least at first. Making each omelet takes about thirty seconds. If you're left-handed, of course you just reverse the whole hand procedure. The omelet is perfect for brunch just as it is. Or you might want to make it into a ham omelet, cheddar cheese, chicken livers, fines herbes, bacon, or put into it any other kind of fillings that egg cookbooks offer. As for the ideal omelet pan, there isn't any; Mr. Stanish used cast aluminum, but you can use an iron pan, or enamel, or one of the no-stick pans, or perhaps a copper-bottomed pan, which is the kind I use. Ideally the pan should be about seven inches across the bottom and have curved sides.

Whatever you decide to make for a Sunday brunch, choose something simpler than you think you can handle. You can always make something more complicated later on. If you like the idea of inviting friends for Sunday brunch but would rather not even scramble an egg yourself, you may be lucky enough to find a place that will cater a breakfast for you, but you can expect it to cost you an astronomical price. If you live in a big city, you may be luckier. One live-alone news magazine researcher who lives in Manhattan's East 80s and who works until late on Saturdays claims she has no time to shop even for brunch food. So on Saturday evening she goes to the famous Goldberg's Pizzeria and buys a "Goldilocks," which is a pizza made of cream cheese and lox. She heats it in her oven on Sunday noon and her guests sit around blissfully eating their hot Goldilocks, which is preceeded by a dish of mixed fruits (bought frozen, then thawed), and followed by hot coffee in mugs.

Of course you can also buy already-frozen pizza dough in the supermarket and make your own Goldilocks or breakfast variations thereof. But whatever new dish you do decide on, test it out in advance on yourself, since it might be a disaster, and a disaster in private is less discomfiting than ruining a brunch for a half-dozen guests. Testing in advance is a rule for whatever entertaining you do, of course, since you can sorely try a friendship by confusing a guest with a guinea pig.

Then there is the cocktail party, which sounds like a very good idea, but which unfortunately doesn't do anything worthwhile in the way of sprucing up a live-aloner's social life. I am taking the trouble to mention the cocktail party only to save you the time you might otherwise waste on it, in case you have some vague notion in the back of your mind that it is a good idea; and it is only fair to tell you why it isn't. Or perhaps you are already wasting your time giving cocktail parties. In either case, one drawback in giving a cocktail party is the impossibility of deepening a friendship with anyone you've met and would like to know better, just by inviting him (or her) to your apartment to mingle and drink with a lot of other people. You might as well be a near-invisible bartender. Beyond a "Hello," or a few mechanical civilities, there's no chance in the cocktail party hubbub for an honest, relaxed exchange of ideas or news, or to develop any understanding or warmth. The same thing often seems to go for your cocktail party guests, vis-à-vis each other. "It's frustrating," is the way one successful young career woman in television once over lunch described her feelings to me. "You meet people, you want to talk about something, and all you get back is stereotyped role-playing conversation. Cocktail party conversation. It's stillborn." Another friend complains of being always embarrassed at cocktail parties because "I never know whose elbow to stand at and listen," and still another friend, who is a cosmopolitan and interesting man, nevertheless confesses that he gets an impatient feeling, at a cocktail party, of being "locked out" of various conversations around him. It isn't difficult, either, to spot an ordinarily self-assured friend who has developed the rigid, alarmed look of a wallflower, the Nobody-is-going-to-talk-to-me-and-everybody-sees-it look. Naturally, all this doesn't help much to further what you're entertaining people for, which is to enrich your social life by having people in to enjoy themselves so much they'll be eager to ask you back. It doesn't help, either, that cocktail party hors d'oeuvres are fattening but not satisfying, and that the party ends leaving guests to go away hungry, but after all those highballs or cocktails hardly able to cook dinner; so out of desperation some of them eat in restaurants that are shockingly expensive or else cheap and unattractive. Of course some won't eat at all, and will drink too much often simply to kill hunger pangs, and will have a Morning After, and won't like you any the better for it. Neither will those guests who linger overlong, eating leftover canapés and hoping you'll open a can of spaghetti or something; they won't be any more your partisan the next day even if you do feed them something. They'll be too ashamed of themselves for having hung on.

There are, of course, some hostesses who invite guests to cocktail parties to "pay back" invitations or to get rid of business or other bothersome social obligations. This is about as friendly and hospitable as dropping a pail of water on somebody's head. It is also a waste of money—cocktail parties are hideously expensive, what with liquor and hors d'oeuvres costing what they do. And worse, it is a waste of your time and effort to have a party with no warmth and no love, a cold-hearted party. It makes a lot more sense to decide that anybody you like well enough to invite to your home, you like well enough to offer relaxation, good conversation, and good solid food. To do less is to ask them in only to turn them out into the blizzard, à la Little Eva. And how good a social paste is that?

One of the best social pastes for a live-aloner is a buffet supper —informal, heart-warming, and naturally with delightful things to eat. You can feed a lot of people at a buffet supper, and they'll all relax with their drinks, knowing they're going to be well fed in due course. A buffet supper is easy and fun, and it's also inexpensive, since ethnic foods are in and you can easily become expert and even famous for one or two ethnic specialities—spaghetti and meatballs, Mexican enchiladas and tacos, chicken paprikash. You can make a reputation with Greek moussaka, Hungarian goulash, or curried meatballs. Pick a dish out of a magazine or cookbook and make it yours. A Turkish dish like *imam bayildi,* which in Turkish means "The Priest Fainted" (he fainted with ecstasy when he tasted the dish, because it was so delicious) sounds intimidatingly difficult and even suspiciously expensive (one story is that the priest fainted twice—the second time when his wife told him what the ingredients had cost). But actually *imam bayildi* is a mixture of mostly eggplant, tomatoes and onions, and is easy enough to make after a little practice. Good and easy-to-serve buffet dishes are things like Chinese shrimp-and-rice, and in fact almost anything you can serve from a chafing dish (for a little extra style). Leaf through any of the twenty-five chafing-dish books available and you'll certainly find some recipes you like.

There's nothing like your own ethnic background, too, to give you more identity to guests. Anya, a twenty-two-year-old Norwegian friend of mine who is with an American-Norwegian newspaper, started out dispiritedly serving buffets of what she hoped was "American" cooking, but she was so hopelessly inept at it that she gave it up and resorted to Norwegian dishes. She promptly became more of a Somebody. If you've moved to another part of the United States, you can be just as successful with a regional dish from back home—baked beans from Boston, shrimp remoulade if you're from New Orleans, and so on.

A good plan is to have two main dishes on the buffet table, at least one of them hot, some kind of salad and possibly hot bread or rolls. A simple dessert and coffee finishes off the meal. To be really considerate, a low-caffeine coffee is also good to have.

Any table does fine as a buffet table—I once even used my desk. Use a card table or use your dining table. Use a chest. Use bookshelves. As for where your guests will stand and sit, remember that your furniture isn't nailed to the floor. Shift it around before guests arrive, so that they can form comfortable conversational groups, some sitting and some standing, as they choose, while they have drinks and the simplest of hors d'oeuvres such as an interesting cheese or two and bowls of crackers. When it comes time to serve the buffet one choice is to set up two or three card tables, finding space just about anywhere; if your room is small but you have a foyer, one card table will probably fit into it. I once went to a particularly cozy, candlelit buffet in a three-and-a-half-room apartment. The living room was small so the hostess set up two card tables in the living room and one in her bedroom. Card tables are worth investing in, though of course you can rent them. Or your guests can eat off of whatever end tables you have, and even the coffee table. Etiquette books warn you that guests shouldn't have to eat off plates in their laps, but if you have more guest laps than tables, have them eat off plates in their laps. If it's a question of laps as against a forest of matchstick-legged tables, I prefer laps. I find that men do, too.

Buffet serving is easy; you can do the dishing out alone, or have a friend help you. But later when people go back for seconds, they're on their own.

One good way to give a buffet supper is to invite people for 6:30, let them enjoy their drinks and conversation for an hour or so, and serve the buffet around 7:30 or 8:00. That leaves time for the evening to wind up and everyone to depart by midnight, which is nice if it's a week night and you and your guests have to go to work next day. On a Friday or Saturday, though, you might turn it into a late-night supper: Invite people for around 8:30 when they'll have had a light supper at home and are comfortably replete. They'll be hungry by 11:30, and maybe even ravenous, what with their appetites sparked by the drinks, and you can serve the buffet then.

When you live alone, you'll of course have people in to dinner, just like anybody else. You know all about dinner. Six, seven, or eight people is ideal. Give them cocktails or highballs, and simple appetizers, and don't let them wait more than an hour before feeding them. If you feed them well on viands that are interesting and reasonably well prepared, and give them wine to go with it, conversation will flow, and they will have a good time, and you will end up with five to seven friends who can't help but be fonder of you than when they arrived.

One way to see that your dinners are tasty is to take a cooking course, which is an expensive method. Another, that won't cost anything but your time, is to learn the basics out of a cookbook, experimenting and accumulating a small but good repertoire. It is a good idea to have a party file folder, so you'll know to whom you fed what dishes last time, and in which you can keep a record of what you spent, the amount you had to buy, what went particularly well, and what was a terrible mistake.

As for what dishes you serve food on, no live-aloner of any

style or sophistication these days has to worry about not having a big enough set of matching dishes. Everybody mixes china. If you have only six colored plates or plates with designs, you can alternate them with six pure white plates from one of the many inexpensive Chinese stores. Alternate plaids and polka dots, blue with yellow plates, plain-colored with patterned. An interior designer friend of mine not only mixes plates but gets fresh, stunning effects by mixing two colors of candles in a candelabra, and sometimes three. As for tablecloths for a dinner, mainly restaurants seem to be using them lately, almost everyone else uses pretty table mats of anything from cork to tapa cloth to grass. And paper napkins of good quality are practically standard, so that takes care of laundry problems.

Serving liquor is another story entirely. You can't be casual about how to mix drinks, not if you're going to mix good ones. And mixing good drinks is vital. Nothing will start an evening off better than a very good drink, and few things will defeat it like bad drinks. A surprising number of people assume that mixing cocktails and highballs demands an expertise that only the male mind can apprehend. This might be because the man, as host and head of the household, has always had the job of mixing. I can think of any number of girls and women I know who have never mixed a drink, including some live-aloners who were married twenty years or more.

But when you live alone, you're both host and hostess. It is true—and you can depend on it—that some considerate male guest will always offer to help you with the bar duties. Or he'll even offer to take over completely. Right out of your hands. *Presumably* he knows how to mix good drinks. But then again he may not. A good heart and willing hands can nevertheless mean too much vermouth in the martini, and even (it has happened) gingerale in the Scotch, and there will be a lot of downcast faces among your guests. Why take the risk? Then, too, it hardly seems fair to turn this much of the job over to a guest. Any live-aloner should, in any case, know how to mix and serve good drinks. Being knowledgeable about mixing highballs and cocktails is true hospitality.

There's no mystique about mixing drinks. All you need is the liquor, some minimum equipment, minor ingredients, and a good little booklet of drink recipes. The easiest method for serving drinks at a party is to clear a good-sized table, desk, or chest in the living room (ahead of time, of course) and put all your drink supplies on it, instead of trying to carry drinks from the kitchen. The basic supplies to set out are the liquor and an ice bucket, and it's a good idea to make plenty of ice cubes in advance, putting them in plastic bags until you have plenty in the freezer. You'll also need a jigger for measuring, and a bottle opener, and your paring knife (for lemon peel). For the cocktails, you'll need a mixing pitcher and long-handled spoon and a shaker; also a bottle of bitters. For highball mixers, you'll need tonic and club soda, and perhaps tomato juice in case someone wants a Bloody Mary. Diet cola is fine for nondrinkers. The other ingredients are olives and onions for martinis, plus any other ingredients your little book says go into any drinks you particularly want to offer your guests. But naturally you don't have to be prepared for everything in the book —you are not, after all, running a cocktail lounge or Harry's Bar, serving Alexanders and Pink Ladies. Anyway, most guests will want a highball or the simplest and driest cocktail, since these go best before a buffet or dinner. In case there are some sherry lovers around, you might want to keep a good sherry on hand, preferably Spanish, like Tio Pepe, which is dry and delicate and which is best slightly chilled.

Have plenty of everything, since none of these ingredients wears out, dries up, or goes bad, and eventually you're going to entertain again. If there's leftover tomato juice, have it for breakfast. If you're worried about investing too much in liquor, arrange with the liquor store to take back unopened bottles.

You can get fifteen good drinks out of a quart of liquor. At three drinks for each guest, if you have ten people, that's two bottles of liquor. That doesn't really tell you much, since you're never sure who's going to want what kind of liquor. It is possible for all the guests to want vodka when you have one bottle of vodka and one of Scotch. One thing you can depend on, though, is that in winter people prefer Scotch and in summer vodka or gin and tonic, at least generally. The kind of liquor you should have on hand is the kind that's most popular in your part of the country. In some parts of the South, and across the country, it will be bourbon. In New York, and on the West Coast, about half your guests will want Scotch and the rest generally want vodka, with a few wanting gin. For security, you should keep on hand a bottle of rye and perhaps a bottle of Canadian whiskey. This means you'll have a cellar of five or six different bottles of liquor, plus a bottle of dry vermouth for martinis and sweet vermouth for Manhattans.

Having made an investment in all this (or some of it) you may be in for a shock when some guests ask simply for a glass of white wine or red wine. It happens more and more lately. In the most sophisticated New York to Los Angeles circles, guests want wine, and in unsophisticated circles they want wine, and you will feel chagrined if you don't have a half-gallon of a reasonably good domestic white or red wine on hand. It is nice to have all these things in the closet. But if your budget can't stand it, firmly offer your guests one wine and a choice of two or three kinds of liquor, or any one of the many drinks that you can make from your two or three bottles. And don't worry about it. If you don't, they won't.

Making a good drink is not, by the way, the same thing as making a generous drink. It is better not to be overly generous. A newly divorced woman friend of mine who lives in Seattle has recently begun to give parties, and writes me enthusiastically that her theory for a successful party is to immediately give an arriving guest a stiff drink. "I meet them at the door and immediately provide them with a *triple* drink," she writes, "to make sure they have a good time." One of her recent guests not long ago wrote me that he'd gone to one of her parties but didn't know for sure what it had been like. "She met me at the door," his letter related, "and gave me a drink right away; and that's the last I remember."

As for quality, in shopping for liquor, ask a man friend who knows liquor, and trust his judgment. He'll often, for instance, say he knows a good quality Scotch or gin that is less expensive but as good as a more expensive brand. If he says so, believe him. You have to believe somebody, and if it's a choice between taking the advice of a liquor-store dealer (until you get to know him) or a knowledgeable friend, choose the friend's.

Once you've expertly mixed the highball or cocktail, the thing to serve it in is a glass made out of glass, and never, if you are wise, out of plastic. You've gone to all the trouble of offering your guests a style, a mood, an evening that includes soft lights, good food, well-made drinks—all the sensory pleasures. Glass, the weight and feel and clink of it, carries out the mood. You don't have to have cut-glass tumblers and clear crystal from Baccarat but it's worth it to invest in some reasonably good glasses in a couple of shapes—highball glasses and old-fashioned glasses can be used for just about any drink.

You'll be more successful at entertaining if you do it in a way that fits your own personal style. A young Vermonter, who came to New York three years ago right out of college, freezes with fear at the idea of inviting a half-dozen people to sit down to a proper dinner. But she has solved her entertainment problem by buying a little butane cooking unit and informally cooking at the table. She has learned to make all kinds of delicious things for a dozen people or so. She'll buy shrimp and let each guest cook his own shrimp tempura, dipping the shrimp in batter and then cooking it in the hot fat for a couple of minutes until it rises to the top, crisp and brown. She comes of a large family and says she feels most at home with lots of people, all claiming it's their turn at the cooking pot. And she's most at ease with the fun and commotion. Guests sit wherever they please, and some don't bother to sit at all. If you're the informal type too, and like cooking at the table, you can try everything from Japanese cooking with a wok to making Swiss Fondue, in which case your guests do sit together around the cooking pot but don't have to wait their turn, they can all put their fondue forks in the pot. Since beer is usually the drink with this informal sort of eating, this kind of entertaining is inexpensive. Someone once said that the best parties are given by people who can't afford them. Perhaps they had this informal kind of entertaining in mind.

What will make your guests love you more is a little consideration for their waistlines. Since most people are either overweight or dieting, they'll be grateful if you don't present them with irresistible but fattening foods about which they'll later feel guilty. Consideration, in general, will get you far—even consideration as seemingly minor as breaking up salad greens into small enough pieces for a guest to fit them into his mouth instead of serving pieces sized for the giant in *Jack and the Beanstalk*. Any number of other little considerations help tremendously in making your guests become your partisan. For one thing, tell them how informal or dressy the evening will be, even go so far as to tell them what you're planning to wear yourself—and then don't change your mind and betray them; it won't be appreciated if you tell them to come casually dressed and that you're wearing wool slacks, only to have them arrive in wool slacks and find you wearing a silk Pucci. Being specific about the day and date and hour they're expected is vital. It is enough that people go through some anxiety wondering if they have the day right; it is much worse if, instead of arriving next Wednesday at 8:30, they erroneously arrive on this Wednesday and find you washing your hair. Also (as too many of us discover too late) if you're going to call your guests to change a party date or cancel it because you've suddenly come down with the flu, or for some other good reason, the only person you should deliver the message to on the telephone should be the person you've invited, *not* their secretary or their mother, or someone who happens to have been passing by their ringing office telephone at lunchtime when everybody is out, and who promises to deliver the message. Inadvertently undelivered messages result in all sorts of embarrassments, enmities, and relationships that are shattered just when they're in the most delicate, formative stage. And tell your guest what to expect in the way of food. And at approximately what time the food will be served. These two bits of advice sound ridiculously unnecessary, but it's amazing how often guests are uncertain just what the hostess intends. I remember one evening last winter being invited to visit a friend who occasionally has a couple of people in for drinks during the evening, only to discover when I arrived that this time she had meant dinner but hadn't said so. Since she had also neglected to tell the other four people she'd asked, her dinner went uneaten, and the chagrin was general. If you *don't* intend to feed people, make that plain, too. If it's just cheese and crackers, say so. Nothing helps keep the air clearer than being explicit, and people are much more comfortable when they know the situation exactly. For the same reason, if a guest asks if he or she can bring a gift, be honest about what you'd like. And choose something they'll have the satisfaction of seeing you use—flowers, a wine (tell them whether you want red or white, whichever suits the food better), candles that you can burn at each end of a buffet table or elsewhere in the room. It will also save them from wasting their money on something you can't use and end up by sticking away in a closet.

A little consideration for yourself is worth paying attention to, also, since it will make you feel more congenial toward your guests, and consequently will make you more charming. Have whatever is going to make things easier for you, such as an electric knife, or a sizable electric griddle that makes eight pancakes at once for a brunch. If once a year you want to give a sizable buffet supper, consider having a maid in for four hours to keep the kitchen clean, keep used glasses and dishes cleared away and fresh ones put out, and maybe to serve the coffee and clean up afterward. Or a once-a-week cleaning woman, if you have one, may be willing to stay a couple of extra hours and help you out, for which you pay her time and a half. If you hate having anyone else around to help, or your salary doesn't cover this much expense, then prepare everything possible in advance so you won't be spending your time in the kitchen. And the more physically comfortable you are, the better. Even for an informal evening, you're bound to be both active and a little anxious, and that makes for warmth; so it's wise to wear something you won't get too hot in. If wool next to your skin will shortly make you feel like a monk in a hair shirt, avoid it.

We've barely mentioned serving wine at dinner, but it is worth talking about because there is something remarkably hospitable and often very elegant about wine with dinner. Unfortunately any number of people are fearful they'll serve the wrong wine in the wrong way, thereby revealing some terrible social inadequacy, and then of course the world will come crashing down on top of them, and they might as well be dead anyway. A plethora of wine snobs have made too many of us feel this way. Of course, that is nonsensical. It is foolish to be intimidated by wine snobs. People in other countries drink wine as casually as they drink tea or coffee, and don't carry on about the fine points. Of course, you may already be knowledgeable about buying and serving a bottle of wine; but if not, the few things to know are simple.

Basically you should know that white wines are served chilled, and you can chill your bottle (or bottles) in the refrigerator for a couple of hours, or in an ice bucket or even in a big salad bowl or cooking pot for about twenty minutes, surrounded by plenty of ice cubes and some water. Dry white wines are light and delicate, so serve them with light and delicate foods, since strong foods will overpower them so thoroughly that you won't be able to taste them. You simply use your head about this—white wines go well, for instance, with seafood, ham, veal, chicken, and other delicate foods, but not if you turn the chicken into a chicken cacciatore that is overpoweringly rich and strong. And you can see that a dry white wine might very well be delicious with cold sliced beef, since cold sliced beef is relatively delicate. So use your taste buds and your judgment. You treat pink wines, which are the rosés, exactly the same as white wines: chill them, remember they're delicate, and use your head. There are also *sweet* white wines. They go with dessert. If you can afford to serve one, it will make your guests feel blissfully satisfied.

As for red wines, serve them at room temperature. Or serve them a little cooler, if you like warm rooms. A *little* cooler means fifteen minutes in the refrigerator, at the most. Red wines are mostly dry, and here again you use your judgment. The lighter red wines taste delightful with lighter foods like veal and other light meats, but naturally the heavier red wines taste better with heavier foods. There are a handful of foods that are unfriendly to *any* wine, red or white, and you'll simply be wasting your money if you serve wine with them: these are strong foods, principally onions and garlic, anchovies, or kippers. A vinegary salad, spicy curries, and mustard aren't any better. . . . But all these go beautifully with ice-cold beer.

If you have a few people in to dinner, uncork your wine in

the kitchen, using one of those blessedly easy corkscrews that lever the cork up without any muscle power (you can buy one in any good hardware store) and the bottle then goes on the table in front of the host's seat, or in the live-aloner's case, in front of her seat. Since we have entered the world of Ms., I see no reason to designate a male guest as the "host," as women have always been inclined to do. This is your home, these are your guests. Of course, if you feel it will make some particular male happier, or at least keep him from feeling anxious, you may want to let him pour. Otherwise, as I was saying, place the bottle on the table in front of *your* seat. You won't really have to taste it first at the table (or he won't) as is generally done in a restaurant, since if there was anything wrong with the wine you found that out in the kitchen by smelling the cork. If it smells like the cork it's a bad bottle, but if it smells like the wine, it's good. The perfect glass for any wine is a tulip-shaped champagne glass, and it's best to have clear glass, not colored, so that your guests can enjoy the color of the wine. It's ideal if the glass holds at least eight ounces. When you pour, you fill the glass only half full so that your guests can swirl it around in the glass and admire it and the wine can "breathe"—that is, exposing it to air is supposed to develop the wine's bouquet, by evaporation. In fact, when you're having a red wine, you might want to open the bottle a half hour or an hour ahead of time, so it can have more time to "breathe" and develop a better taste. This doesn't work with chilled white wines, though, so you open them just before you serve them.

When it comes to buying your wine, pick the most reputable and knowledgeable store you know of, tell them whether you want a light dry red, or whatever, and trust their judgment until you get to know wines. As for costs, you know your own pocketbook and what you can spend. One friend of mine who likes to have an occasional wine-and-cheese party, buys a whole gallon of excellent quality wine for about nine dollars. But when she is low in funds she buys a gallon of good wine for four dollars. If you like a touch of elegance, you can buy a quart bottle of any number of delicious imported or domestic wines for about $2.50 to four dollars, though of course you can spend considerably more if you want more esoteric wines. If you buy a case of any kind of wine, the salesman will usually give you 10 percent off. It's fun and enlightening to discuss the wine with the salesman. It is also good to keep a record of what you paid for it, either on a slip of paper in back of your cookbook, or in a little notebook, noting whether or not you liked it, and so on. No one can remember much about wines unless it's a hobby. Assuming you're not a wine specialist, gourmet, wine snob, or a member of Chevaliers du Tastevin, the simplest thing is to own a little handbook on wines and keep it beside your cookbooks for reference. An unpretentious and simple paperback like the Alexis Bespaloff *Signet Book of Wine* (which is the one I use) is fine for glancing into when you need a refresher.

If you become enamored of serving wines, you can even go on to starting a wine cellar. The expression "wine cellar" sounds intimidating, but the floor of your bedroom closet or a coat closet makes a very good wine cellar (since it is dark and relatively cool) and the bottles should lie on their sides (so the cork won't dry out and let air in), and a wine rack that holds eight bottles costs about $3.50—and that's about all you have to know about wine cellars. You can have an excellent one of thirty bottles for about one hundred dollars, or you can have a bottle or two of wine on hand, and consider it your wine cellar. A bottle or two on hand is a very nice thing to have, in case you'd like impulsively to ask a friend or two to drop in some Sunday afternoon when liquor shops are closed. Once when I was working in Paris for three weeks, on an assignment, a Frenchwoman who ran a photography agency invited me and three other people to her apartment on a Sunday afternoon, and ever since then I have been convinced that one of the best ways to spend a late summer Sunday afternoon is on a dusty balcony eating raspberries and drinking a glass of chilled white wine. My New York apartment has no balcony but my living room faces south and is sunny, and I sometimes ask two or three people in for this kind of Sunday afternoon repast.

It is positively amazing how much more favorably and even lovingly you can view life and society, once you start entertaining and being entertained in return.

CHAPTER 8

Friends

Certain friends can be good for you when you live alone, but others can do you no more good than Iago did Othello.
  Of course, you need a satisfying number of friends and acquaintances, whether your idea of a satisfying number is four or twenty-four. Even if you love to be alone, you have a gregarious side and you will wilt considerably unless you have enough friends to go to the movies or theater with, or talk with on the telephone, or even go for a walk with. Maybe you will never feel you have enough friends and will feel occasional twinges of loneliness . . .

but a reasonable aim is to have at least a few friends for enjoyable social activities.

But *which* friends? A lot depends on which friends. It is advisable first to take a good look at the friends you already have. If you are divorced, widowed, or over thirty, you may have already discovered in your very first month of living alone that, yes, even in the 1970s, you have at least one married old friend (I had three) who is well-meaning but determined to believe that you are lonely, miserable, and totally at loose ends. When a friend like this invites you to dinner, even if you arrive looking as glamorous as Lauren Bacall in *Applause,* your hostess's manner will shortly convey to the other guests that you are really Little Orphan Annie and to be pitied. Your live-alone state is equivalent, in her mind, to being excluded from the world . . . into whose grace she has kindly reintroduced you, at least for the evening. Ludicrous as this is, it is almost impossible (and I know it well) to weather such persistent sympathy without ending feeling embarrassed, chagrined, irritated, and more than faintly demoralized. That's true even though you know very well that your live-alone life is happier, more adventurous, more enjoyable, and altogether more satisfying than your hostess's. Even a modicum of this old-fashioned friendship is bad for one's morale. The only thing to do with old friends like this (and relatives, too) who persist in feeling sorry for you, is to retrain them. I admire the rather unusual but effective retraining method of one new widow. Forty-four, humorous, chic, and with an interesting job, she was nevertheless possessed of a couple of relatives (aunt and uncle) who worried at her with all kinds of anxious phrases. "Telephone us if you need us," they would say, ". . . or drop in." After some months of this depressing sympathy, and having neither telephoned nor dropped in, she decided to telephone—to ask them if they'd mind looking after her dog while she went to a weekend party in Connecticut. And twice in one week she had a florist erroneously deliver flowers to their address (they had the same last name) instead of her own. She even, one Sunday morning, arrived at their apartment in a taxi, which she kept waiting, to borrow a bottle of Napoleon brandy. If this sounds pretty extreme, and a lot of effort, at least it worked. Her relatives have come to think of her as leading a glamorous life; and they now at last have a decent relationship. When you're divorced or widowed, anxious relatives often do come around, in time; they stop hoping, in breathless expectancy, for you to say, "I'm engaged" or, "I'm getting married" when you're only telephoning to ask for the name of that good dentist whose address you lost. They are also becoming at least peripherally aware, in this world of women's liberation, of the Woman's Movement and NOW—so much so that their response to any sprightly marital news might more likely be a disappointed: "What! And give up all that?" But if they are old-fashioned and lachrymose about the whole thing, the less you have to do with them, the better.

A balanced choice of friends, like a balanced meal, is equally important. It is too easy, for instance, for a live-alone woman to fall into the habit of having an overabundance of homosexual men friends. Or at least it's too easy in bigger cities. What's wrong with that is merely that it is often at the sacrifice of other friends, since you have only so much time for socializing. No matter how many attractive qualities homosexual men friends have, no matter how artistic, clever, imaginative, witty, appreciative, and so on homosexual friends may be, you still have the problem of time. I know too many live-alone women who overbalance their social lives this way, often out of laziness. One friend of mine, whenever she is asked by a hostess to bring along a man to dinner, habitually, unthinkingly, invites one of her good homosexual friends to be her escort, when with a little effort she could easily invite a man she's recently met, and who might well find her very attractive if he knew her better (as she might find him), and who in turn would invite her somewhere. It is just as smart to cultivate an assortment of older and younger people, as we suggested earlier—knowing some people who are older and younger adds zest and variety, like a box of assorted chocolates instead of all the same kind.

To be in demand, at all costs, is sometimes tempting, since it keeps your telephone ringing, and when you live alone, it is nice to think that dozens of people out there need you, depend on you, love you. This is a good attitude to get rid of, since it leads to choosing your friends with a wild disregard for quality, in favor of quantity. Moreover, if you want all those people to love you, you in return will have to love them all back, which is time-consuming and impractical. And anyway, you can't make everybody love you. The attempt is as defeating as trying to eat all the strawberry shortcake in the world: It can't be done. Of course, you simply have to learn for yourself when you're going too far in the attempt. Not long ago an acquaintance told me, speaking of a friend of hers, "Margaret had a terrible problem yesterday, an argument with her ex-husband, so I took her in hand and sent her to my analyst for my session." That is a good example of going considerably too far in the attempt (as the analyst undoubtedly immediately informed her). If you have that strong a desire to mother any number of stray people as though they were stray dogs and cats, it is better to keep it in check. One other good reason is that, if you don't, you will find yourself so swamped with other people's problems that you'll be hard pressed to find time for your own. Sooner or later you'll resent it and kick over the whole applecart. That is exactly what happened to more than one live-aloner I've met, but particularly to one bright, sympathetic thirty-two-year-old who moved to New York a couple of years ago from my town of Springfield, Massachusetts. From the moment she moved into her own apartment she seemed to be wearing a flashing neon sign that said *You can always come to me when you're in trouble.* People did. They even took to calling her up long distance, sober or sodden, reversing the charges, telling her their troubles, and her telephone bill became catastrophic. She began to look pretty exhausted, too, but luckily she went off to Europe on a two-week vacation, and when I ran into her a couple of months later she looked relaxed and happy. What had happened? While in Europe, she had been in a shop in Madrid picking out presents for all those friends when, as she told me, "Suddenly I realized I didn't want to buy them anything—I didn't even like to *think* about them." Faced with this surprising revelation, and having a little time to herself to think about it, she decided that she wasn't living her own life, or, as she put it, "I was just an observer, taking care of all of *them.*" Back home again in New York she weeded out the people on whom she felt she was wasting all her energy. She now has energy, but she is going through the slow (but at least positive) process of making some real friends. It isn't easy to give up even a friend or two, particularly if people aren't banging your door down to be friends. But if you're among those who have been accumulating a gaggle of problem-ridden friends, it is worth taking the step. It is also not an easy step, if you've fallen into this particular trap, because you've had the advantage of feeling superior; in contrast to the miseries of your friends you can feel you have very few problems indeed. There is something to be said for contrasts like this (it is nice to feel superior) but not much. You're better off with friends who can offer more worthwhile friendships than this; it's eventually more satisfying.

As for friends in general, when you live alone and have only a few friends or a couple of "best" friends, you're putting all your eggs in one basket. If you have only three friends and one suddenly goes off to live in Los Angeles or gets a job in Alaska and another marries and moves to Houston, there you are with a big gap in your life. You need enough other friends on hand to fill in the gap, like a river rushing in to fill a dry area. It wouldn't matter so much if you lived with a housemate or two, or in a swirl of family members (or even a hippie commune) where there are plenty of people in the household to provide a variety of social interminglings. But when you live alone, your friendships are more direct, with nobody in between to water them down: They have more value; each person counts; each departure is felt. This, by the way, is true of enemies, too. It is even worthwhile to cultivate a few. There is nothing like a couple of worthwhile enemies to add zest to life and keep you knowing exactly who you are. As an early Leonard Bacon poem has it, "I have an enemy, and I praise God/ I hate him to his pudgy finger-tips./ . . . What would I do without him? He renewed/ Valor within my miserable soul,/ self-reverence, self-knowledge, self-control,/ And other old, unhappy, far-off things./ And I, because a rooting swine was lewd,/ found myself launched on unaccustomed wings."

Maybe you already have plenty of friends and acquaintances (and enemies), but if you haven't there are any number of ways to acquire them. It takes effort, but it is at least easier than acquiring a good French accent. You can't, though, wait, immobile, for them to come and find you—even Muhammad finally gave up and went to the mountain. In a small town, you have dozens of places to meet people, and in a bigger city, hundreds. You can take courses in everything from jewelry-making to yoga to Hungarian cooking. You can take a course to create something, to learn something, to develop your taste in anything from medieval music to modern poetry, and thereby meet people with similar interests. If you're shy, you're far better off choosing a course that involves you with other people in a class, so that you have a built-in reason for chatting and becoming friends. The twenty-two-year-old cousin of a friend of mine joined a film-making class at New York University, and during the whole first semester was too shy to speak to anyone, and was monosyllabic when anyone spoke to her. But in the second semester she found that the procedure was for the class to break up into teams of four people, each team to make a "film," one as producer, another as director, and so on. You can't argue and discuss and plan anything with other people without getting involved, and two of her close friends grew out of that little team. Acting classes are another good choice if you're a laggard about breaking the ice. Meeting people is never enough; you can go to an Italian class for a year and come away fluent in the subjunctive, but without becoming friends with anybody in the class unless you make some advances. Lots of people who live alone feel they have to pretend they're not interested in meeting people; so after a class or a political meeting or a tenants' committee rally, they smile a cool goodnight. It is important to get over the feeling that it would be hopelessly mortifying to admit that you want to make friends; that you're friendly and interested. Certainly you risk being rebuffed. But a few rebuffs needn't put you off, though I remember once being crushed by an advertising woman who, when I suggested one evening after an art class that we stop for a coke, suspiciously inquired if I wanted a job with her ad agency.

As for meeting people through other activities in your city or town, if you take the trouble to keep an eye on the newspapers you can discover an amazing number of opportunities. Lately, in New York, for instance, you can even go on Saturday morning walking trips, or join an inexpensive bicycle group tour (you bring your own lunch), or even, if you're rich enough, join one of the "Discover New York" tours that are guided tours for up to twelve people, including a picnic lunch and getting from here to there in a Mercedes-Benz bus, at costs of from $8.50 to $12.00. If you keep an ear to the ground, whatever your town or city, you'll run into any number of possibilities for fun and meeting people. I insist here, too, that you're more likely to meet people if you join a friendly group in a give-and-take situation, or some activity. I understand from things I've read that you can meet people if you wander dreamily and romantically through art galleries and museums, but I don't believe it. I've never met anyone who developed a friendship that way (except once, and it was a friendship that came to no good).

If you're enterprising, you might even start something yourself; instead of being the tail on the kite, be the kite. Start a tenants' committee if you think your apartment building needs one, start a bridge club if you're a bridge addict and can't find a club. My dentist's older sister lives in a small Pennsylvania town, loves the theater, and started a repertory theater group; it hasn't made a dime in four years (since it started, in fact), but she has made so many friends and acquaintances that she hardly ever gets to New York to visit her brother, and he complains that when she does come she is too busy to see him anyway, since she comes with her group of theater-minded friends and they have advance tickets to all the shows.

Even taking a temporary, off-beat kind of job can be worth considering; the most exceptional case I can think of involves a girl assistant at a natural history museum. She is new to the city, sociable, knows few people as yet, likes children, and is generally broke because she doesn't know how to cook and therefore eats most of her meals out. Because of all these circumstances, when she saw a newspaper ad for a fund-raising job that would last two months and would raise money for a blind children's organization, she decided to moonlight, applied for the job, and got it. During those nine weeks of fund-raising, which consisted of visiting a list of assorted rich folk and millionaires to persuade them to contribute to the fund, she met a number of pleasant people. A couple of them are at least friendly enough to ask her occasionally to their sizable and glamorous Long Island weekend summer parties. She is not shy about going, either, and she enjoys herself, and has met a few more people while out there.

Shyness, by the way, can be a weighty problem if you're new to living alone on the heels of becoming a divorcée or widow. You are liable to worry that people are merely being polite or sorry for you. It is better simply to take people at their face value: that is, if they invite you for dinner or elsewhere, it is reasonable to assume that they are not merely being polite, but that they really like you and want you. Nobody *made* them invite you. It seems a long time ago (but was seven years ago) when one July day I went up to the swimming pool on the roof of my apartment building, and a nearby friendly group of sun-worshipers offered me a gin-and-tonic from their thermos, I had to suppress an impulse to say, "No, thanks" and leap into the swimming pool because I assumed they were just being "nice" to a new widow. Who knows?—maybe they were (some day I must ask them; they are now my friends). But you have to start somewhere, and the where is by responding.

You are bound to attract a friend or acquaintance or two if you develop some sort of an interest or a hobby that matches theirs. If you know something about early American dolls or antiques, for instance, your scouting around for them can turn up friends with kindred interests who are also scouting in antique shops or at American doll shows. A hobby needn't be expensive, either. Even if you own only one rickety Shaker rocking chair, it gives you a jumping off place for a thousand conversations concerning myths, history, lore, old-time machine tools, and so on. It also makes you an Authority. Some people, if you think about it, have become authorities on such minor subjects as where George Washington slept or didn't sleep. You can become an authority on W. C. Fields or Egyptian pyramids, or on graffiti (there is even a course on graffiti, past and present, at the New School in New York). And you can, moreover, charge any number of courses on your credit card. Or what about poster art? Or food? Becoming interested in food had a lot to do with bettering the life of one woman I can point to, a well-off divorcée in her forties who moved from Evansville, Indiana, to New York right after her divorce. She had no consuming passion or even hobby, unless you could call drinking quantities of very dry martinis a hobby. After close to a year of this, she had a near physical breakdown, and her doctor got the idea through to her that her alcoholic consumption was replacing food, and that if she knew what was good for her she'd go after better nutrition. Her answer to that was to order a half-dozen *haute cuisine* cookbooks, on the theory that if she had to eat she was going to do it elegantly, with wine. The cookbooks fascinated her, and she enrolled in a Cordon Bleu cooking school. Gradually she worked up to becoming an expert cook and even a rather snobbish gourmet. Before long, she had joined a group of fellow cooking snobs who once a week go to dinner at each other's homes, to approve or sneer. It is all a life-and-death matter, and since a true gourmet would rather fling himself off a cliff than hold a martini glass in his hand before a meal, and since strong liquor is ruinous to the palate, her liquor consumption has slid back down to almost nothing (so have her hips). She has developed a half-dozen interests related to cookery and today she probably knows as much about mushroom species as any expert. This is a pretty fancy kind of hobby, and quite expensive. But so were the dry martinis.

One good way to meet people is to specialize in something that very few people know anything about, thereby becoming part of a small group of superior-feeling folk. If you become an expert in Swahili, for instance, since almost nobody knows Swahili, you'll be one of a small group, all of whom know all the other Swahili-speaking people around. Or you might even collect something, preferably something very special. A young public relations friend of mine, who for a while handled the India account, collects little talisman figures of Ganesh, the Indian god of good luck—son of Shiva and the goddess Parvati—whose head is shaped like an elephant's and whose elephant trunk you rub for good luck. It gives her a rather special quality and provides her with some wonderful Indian god and goddess legends that fascinate people.

Collecting can even take over your life, if you're not careful (but why not?). At least that's what happened to an older woman, a widow in her mid-fifties whose husband had left her an accounting business which she manages successfully but which she finds unappealing. She is artistic, curious, and prefers the arts to figures. But there she was, that first year, at 6:00 o'clock every evening arriving home to a lonely apartment. Her weekends were particularly unendurable. But she had always been interested in American primitives and early American furniture, and she began shopping around on Saturdays, and gradually collected so much that her apartment finally began to look like that of the Collier brothers. Then one day on her way home from visiting some relatives in Rhode Island, she drove past a tipsy-looking little shop for rent about a dozen miles or so outside of Watch Hill; and of course she rented it. Since then, she spends every weekend transporting her primitive treasures in a station wagon to the country shop where all weekend she sells them. During the week she skips lunch to scout for more gems—crazed china, old spittoons, and so on— on Second Avenue. She has a part-time girl assistant at the Rhode Island shop, some local fame, and an occasional high temperature when she has an exceptionally good day. She is doing a hand-over-fist business, having discovered, as she tells me, that she can buy American antiques cheaper in the big city than in the country, where they came from in the first place; so she makes a profit selling to tourists, with only a small mark-up. And of course she gets her accounting done free.

Being a grasshopper has its attractions too. If you're a dilettante, lured by a dozen different interests instead of sticking with one or two, why not? One of my most pleasurable seasons was a couple of years ago when I spent some winter evenings learning French forms of poetry, like villanelles and so on, and spent weekends going skiing with a busload of people I slowly got to know. That spring, twice a week, I studied hatha yoga with a guru who, astonishingly, could breathe alternately with one lung and then the other, or so it appeared. This is no way to become an expert on anything, but it makes for plenty of diversity and may suit you perfectly. Besides, you can meet a whole spectrum of people. A good plan is to be knowledgeable on one thing (or even an Authority) and at the same time enjoy any number of other interests. Beware of becoming an authority on more than one subject though (or maybe two) or you risk becoming a bore. Nobody wants to hear anyone expound knowledgeably, like a fountain of wisdom, on everything.

You'll attract more people if you create the impression of being somehow "interesting." That sounds like enough to discourage anybody. But it isn't that difficult; or at least it is less difficult than if you live with other people. When you live alone, it's easier to put a more intriguing foot forward. For one thing, you have the advantage of being able to preserve some mystery about yourself. I am thinking of a Maugham-type of tropical island story I once read, involving a mysterious man named Johnson who arrived on the island wearing a black patch over one eye. He intrigued the island society for years, was romantically pursued by all the women, and he kept alive all kinds of fascinating rumors about how he'd lost his eye. No one ever did discover that back home in Wichita, Kansas, he was known as "Crooked Eye" Johnson.

This story has something distinctly in common with the habits of a young woman I know, a successful live-aloner who when she must decline a date makes it a rule never to give an explanation. Phrases like "I have to go to my niece's graduation" are not in her vocabulary; she would prefer to have the other person wonder —and that, in itself, is intriguing. Mystery is a personal right— why not? If you want to take a bath and go to bed at 9:00 P.M., your public doesn't have to know how you spent the evening. One of the most popular, most sought-after live-aloners I know is a woman who goes away one weekend a month, and none of her friends or acquaintances know where. She takes a taxi to the station and that is it. Does she go to visit a country lover? Perhaps she simply goes to an inn, or motel, where she takes naps and recuperates from her job as a legal secretary. Or maybe she is a fishing addict. Or a smuggler. No one knows. But her mystery, though she may be unconscious of it, is very effective.

Or perhaps you have a more romantic or colorful concept of yourself than you've been daring to show. If so, why not indulge it? It is better to be a little offbeat and odd, rather than dull—as a Portuguese friend of mine decided. In fact she is not really Portuguese; she is actually from Massachusetts, but she fell in love with Portugal when she was thirteen and spent three high school years there, when her engineer father worked there. She has a Portuguese motif in her two-and-a-half-room apartment, she loves intricate Portuguese jewelry with a history, and she wears her dark hair in a slicked-back hairdo with a bun. She can sing (but not well) two or three of those heart-rending *fado* songs, and an occasional Portuguese exclamation falls from her lips. When she is at a party, people know it—they would never not recall whether she had been there or not. But it is all real, all genuine, since it is the way she feels. If you have an ethnic taste or an urge to release some reined-in part of your personality, you might consider letting it expand, unfold. Faking it won't work, of course. You can't successfully superimpose something that isn't you, since you can no more turn yourself into a Melina Mercouri by wearing a turban and an enigmatic smile than you can become an astronaut by dressing up in a white space suit and helmet. It is a waste anyway, to try to develop the fake, since the whole point is to develop the real individual that you are.

In line with that, you are more likely to become more effectively "interesting" if you stir up your brains a little—go to a poetry-reading, see a play, take in a movie, spend an evening with a news magazine. Take sides on pornography, wars, capital punishment—take any side, it doesn't matter. Curl up with a new best seller—and throw it across the room if it exasperates you, and then go out and say so. Even if you're crazy about Jane Austen or inclined to think literature ended with Forster's *A Passage to India,* read a half-dozen new books anyway—it will keep Jane Austen from palling on you—and it will keep you from palling on other people.

Naturally you can't dip into everything, so pick only a handful of things that interest you. You won't be able, anyway, to sustain interest in anything foreign to your personality—unless, of course, you're in love, in which case you will be fascinated by the Mets or the Jets or the economic problems of the Point Barrow natives or archaeological discoveries in Peru, or whether, when you push it out onto the ice it will skate. As a rule, though, if something essentially bores you to the aching point, you'll never be able to talk enthusiastically or intelligently about it. So if you dislike opera, *don't go*. Go to the circus (if you like circuses).

It is not particularly fair (in fact it is not fair at all), but it is a fact that when you meet someone new you're the one who will probably have to start the social wheels turning. You're the one who most of the time will have to suggest plans and places to go. The other person is often too reticent, too busy, or too lazy. You may as well be philosophical about it and do it with good grace; it helps if you keep in mind that it can lead to accumulating a number of good companions for all kinds of social activities.

If you can't gauge a new acquaintance's income level, you can suggest going to something free or inexpensive, which may suit your own pocketbook better too. In New York you can go a thousand places, from the Central Park zoo where you might lunch outdoors on the terrace at cafeteria prices, to the Museum of Modern Art to see the sculpture in the garden after 6:00 P.M. on weekends when the garden gate is open without admission charge. Or you can call the Free Events in New York information telephone number, which is 472-1003 and find out about all the indoor and outdoor free programs you can go to in parks, libraries, museums, and streets. Then pick one and suggest it. Or if you can afford it, pay at the Modern Art to see old movies like *Getting Gertie's Garter* or *Rebecca of Sunnybrook Farm* with Shirley Temple, or an Eisenstein masterpiece like *Potemkin,* or maybe *Up in Mabel's Room*. Or take the three-hour sightseeing cruise around Manhattan and eat hotdogs. In my own upper East Side neighborhood, which is shiny-sophisticated, overlying an older, homey Czechoslovakian culture, occasionally there will be a church supper, and I call up a friend or two and we go and eat homemade Czechoslovakian food, and it is surprising how many other people from the shiny-sophisticated apartments I run into having a good time there, too. Wherever you live, keep an eye out for what's going on, places to suggest to a new acquaintance.

And of course there are sports. If you discover a sport you have in common with a new acquaintance, that's ideal, or if you share an interest in bridge, gin rummy, or symphonies on hi-fi, you've established a *rapport* right there. And *rapport,* in this day and age, is a nice thing to have.

I have neglected so far to mention relatives as a built-in way to meet friends and acquaintances. About all I can say about that is not to neglect them as a source if they're a possible one—but only you can tell about that. In fact, don't neglect any source at hand. At hand is wherever you may be. Two of my good friends are a psychologist and his wife whom I met on a Maine windjammer cruise, another is a writer I met at a travel writers' convention three years ago in Turkey, and a third is a neighbor from whom I borrowed some ice cubes. So there you are.

CHAPTER 9

All
Those
Weekends

Weekends, when you live alone, can be a great pleasure or a slough of despond. Living with another person, if you're bored you can at least be bored in company. But alone, there you are; and if you're not careful, those two beautiful and precious days of leisure can take on the aspect of a nightmare. I have heard that, as far back as the 1920s, the famous psychoanalyst Sandor Ferenczi described something called "weekend neurosis," in which the victim droops around all weekend doing nothing and feeling generally wretched. This is a reasonably accurate description of the complaint of an acquaintance of mine, a spectacularly beautiful model, who nevertheless once confided to me at a party that when she awakens on a Saturday morning, before she even opens her eyes in bed she prays that it is raining—it would be too terrible to be faced with a brilliantly sunny day, since invariably she has made no plans to enjoy it.

To be this planless leaves you liable to a weekend that is inexpressibly dreary and unsatisfying; for to be so at a loss is to eat a boring breakfast without even combing one's hair; to decide that perhaps one ought finally to get dressed—but to go where?; to telephone two or three friends whose phones ring in their empty apartments; to swing the refrigerator door open a dozen times only to be faced with nothing interesting to eat (but to nibble, anyway); to call the beauty salon for a hair appointment in a last desperate effort to give form to a formless day—only to find they are fully booked.

Anyone who suffers through this grim kind of forty-eight hours is simply wasting time. The smart thing to do is to have plans ahead of time, particularly if you're the kind of person who droops all out of shape like ectoplasm without them.

Plans. I am making this point about plans for probably the third time (or is it the fourth?) but it is worth making. Friday night *is* too late to telephone anyone, even for a Saturday afternoon movie. And it is definitely too late for things like suddenly deciding to go off by yourself on a ski trip or a bus trip to see the autumn leaves changing, or wherever your tastes lead you. Friday night is too late to plan for almost anything in the world for a weekend, whether it involves other people or you-on-your-own. This fact is something a lot of us recognize regularly and painfully, generally around 9:00 o'clock on a Friday evening, as though it were brand-new news.

It is easier to make weekend plans if you get rid of any fanciful and unrealistic hope (that so many of us are prey to) that "something wonderful" will happen, that *something wonderful* is right out there and in a minute someone will telephone and invite you for an afternoon drive in the country in his new car. Or to dinner. Or somewhere indefinable. Well, maybe he will and maybe he won't. But the point is not to count on it. Besides, if he does call, it won't hurt if you're not there to accept the last-minute invitation, or you regretfully have to refuse it because you have other plans. If he's interested, he'll call back anyway.

All the equipment anyone needs to get started on satisfying weekends is a calendar, preferably one of those big, flat calendars with an entire month on a page, and space to fill in engagements. It is a great help in seeing instantly what dates and plans you have —everything, in fact, from business to entertainment. Besides planning weekends ahead, it's a good idea to have lots of key plans in advance through the month, like guideposts: theater tickets ahead, classes, movie dates, dinner dates. With a structure like that, you always know where you are. And you have the pleasure of anticipation—lots of it at a glance.

What you plan isn't important. You might want to plan a half-day on Saturday to manicure yourself back to glossiness after the wear and tear of a week at the office, perhaps taking a luxuriously long, perfumed bath. After that, why not a light lunch, and perhaps a leisurely trip to the library or bookstore for a batch of books you've been wanting to read, if you're a reader? The day might include a dinner date (made two weeks ago) with a friend, and on Sunday another set of plans (made two weeks ago). Perhaps it could be a full day's trip. A secretary I know who is crazy about driving and is a nature lover besides, rents a car and drives into the country, always mapping a route to some new spot for lunch. She does this fairly often. Usually she finds someone who's willing to join her. They each pay half the cost of the car, and they return home the same evening. Planning a solid weekend around one interest can even give you a separate "weekend life," as it did for a lab technician in Florida whose weekends were social deserts until she rented a small houseboat for weekends. She splits the cost with another lab technician, and her whole social life is now centered on her houseboat weekends, which are hectic and fun and involve a dozen noisy people, an occasional sunburn, and plenty of ice-cold beer that men guests bring. I have another enthusiastic friend who on weekends is even helping a man she knows build a house on some acreage in New Jersey; the fresh air seems to suit her very well. Fresh air on weekends is a trend right now anyway, and you ought to try it: In New York you can now rise at dawn on weekends and go on all-day or weekend hiking trips with one of the hiking clubs, packing along your own food and drink. Weekends like this are getting so popular that there are now about forty hiking clubs in New York and New Jersey. If that sort of thing appeals to you and you live in that area, call the Sierra Club or write to the New York–New Jersey Trail Conference, P.O. Box 2250, New York City 10001 and they'll send you a list of clubs. If you live in the western part of the country and want that kind of fresh air, write to the Sierra Club, 1950 Mills Tower, San Francisco, California 94104 for the address of your local chapter—and if you live in the east, write to them at 250 West 57th Street, New York City 10019. Every state has a chapter, generally in the most important city. You don't have to be a member of the club, and all you pay for are your transportation and food. You may feel you are back in camp, aged ten, at first. Still, you meet all kinds of people. A secretary in an ad agency, who has been doing this for several weekends, had no transportation at first to get to the meeting place, so the hike leader arranged for her to get a ride with another would-be hiker who turned out to be a young architect; he now picks her up regularly for hike weekends (and sometimes during the week, but not to go hiking). This is a nice bonus, but of course not the sort of thing to count on.

If all that fresh air is too much for you, you can plan your weekend to include activities and new events that are always coming up in every city. Go out—go out with a friend to a concert, a fair, a lecture on Far Eastern philosophy by a man in a turban, go to a free poetry reading, go to a boat show. Stay home enjoyably with a well-planned schedule. Have a weekend destination—or a full-day destination. A friend of mine who lives in Denver loves to gamble, and one weekend out of every month she makes a beeline for Las Vegas (Yes, it is expensive!). Dude ranches are proliferating everywhere, from New Jersey to Montana, so if you've always had a feeling for horses and horseback riding, try spending a weekend riding at a dude ranch. But when it comes to those "singles" resort weekends, to my mind they are depressing and an affront to human dignity, not only to a woman's but to a man's as well, and are good things to avoid.

Live-alone holidays ought to be enjoyable too, but we'd hate to think what the analytical Dr. Ferenczi would say if he could see some of our fellow live-aloners under the duress of a lonely Thanksgiving, Christmas, or New Year's Eve. When you live alone, *maybe* you have relatives nearby who invite you for the holidays, and maybe you haven't. And if you haven't, maybe you're one of the many who hides out, sometimes not even answering the telephone, feeling suicidal, and the first day back at the office saying that, yes, you certainly had a wonderful holiday.

That, of course, is no way to spend a holiday (or any day). If you have no one, and you can't spot any invitations in the offing, a good idea is to invite a batch of people in for a cozy holiday yourself. Call up a few. You'll be surprised how they'll fall on your neck. Some of them have no family either, and others maybe don't have the time, money, or energy to go home to Michigan or Kansas, or Boise, Idaho, where they'd anyway have to cope with flare-ups of sibling rivalry and do dishes after a dinner for fourteen relatives. So there they all are, alone, and why shouldn't they be delighted to come and meet a few people over some drinks and a five-o'clock buffet? Invite them. Invite them for two o'clock and invite one or two couples as well. Eight to ten people, some good conversation, and as the day grows dark, a candlelit buffet is perfect for Christmas or Thanksgiving. Making it a Mexican Christmas with tacos and tamales, or a baked-ham Thanksgiving gives it a bit of spice, an air, a style.

As for New Year's Eve, celebrating with "Auld Lang Syne" and high jinks went out in the early 1960s, and a good place to be at midnight while the New Year is being rung in is sound asleep in bed. You may have other good notions of how to celebrate it, and some of my friends have. If you like to salute the New Year in some way, a good way is to get a night's sleep on New Year's Eve, and then on New Year's Day give a "Recovery" party, as I occasionally do. Three o'clock in the afternoon appears to be the perfect time for many people to begin to face that particular day, so invite guests for that time. Give them something simple. Plain highballs, a five o'clock buffet of plain solid food, and a finish of fresh-brewed hot coffee is a good start for a new year. Everybody goes home early, you clean up and go to bed with a good book.

CHAPTER 10

How to Leave Home... Frequently

Anyone who lives alone and doesn't travel makes us think of a bird sitting in a cage and not noticing that the door is open. Travel fits perfectly into a live-aloner's life. The world is your oyster. If you have not yet recognized this fact, you may still be intimidated by outdated notions about the loneliness of a woman traveling alone. Or perhaps you're simply green about how to travel alone successfully. But that is easily remedied.

It is important to remedy it because every live-aloner ought to go somewhere foreign and exotic as often as possible. You owe it to yourself to feel the hot Caribbean sun or the Mediterranean sun baking into your bare back and shoulders. You owe yourself and your psyche a shady *siesta* in Barcelona, or a *pastis* at a sidewalk café in the South of France, a ferryboat ride from Piraeus to Hydra, or a glimpse of Byzantine art. If you live in Los Angeles, you at least owe yourself a trip to Mexico, and if you haven't yet done that, it is not only a shame, but a tragedy. And if you live in New York, you can buy a vacation in any of a dozen European cities for under three hundred dollars, including your air fare. If you can't afford that much of a trip, you ought to adjust your budget, give up desserts or a new winter coat, or long-distance telephone calls . . . or likely all of them, so that you *can* afford it. It will be worth it.

It will be worth it because travel to strange places is, like proteins and vitamin C and laughter, vital to human life. Art is vital and other cultures are vital, and going somewhere different from where you live, at least once a year, is vital. Even if you don't bring back a single cent (and you won't), you will at least bring back an intoxicating intangible, not to mention a certain sophistication.

If you are not yet doing any of these delightful things, the best way to begin is to disregard all those tiresomely cliché travel folders that show a romantic couple dining by a moonlit Bermuda sea, or walking arm-in-arm down the Via Veneto in Rome, or strolling arm-in-arm along the deck of a cruise ship, and which can leave you thinking nervously: On whose arm will *I* travel? That question is a blood-cousin to many a woman alone's nervous-making: "How will I meet people?" and "What are the dangers?" and "Won't I be lonely?" and similar questions that in letters used to avalanche down on my desk when I was a travel editor.

If you are going to enjoy traveling alone, you will have to recognize that those worries are now as outdated as love beads. Traveling alone in foreign countries isn't any more dangerous than going a block from your apartment at home, provided you handle yourself sensibly (and it's a lot less dangerous than some city blocks I know). And you are not going to be seduced unless you want to be, just like at home.

As for other dangers, yes, the water you drink in one particular country or other had better be bottled water—but the sunset will be a staggeringly beautiful, unforgettable experience. And yes, it will be very hot and dirty in some foreign ports—but you can eat their incredibly juicy peaches and listen to a dressmaker chatter in broken English while she fits you for a dress that she will make in twenty-four hours and that will cost you twenty-five dollars and be worth one hundred and fifty dollars. And yes, it may rain when you're in Florence but when you see Michelangelo's dazzling statue of *David* you won't care about a little rain.

As for being lonely in, say, Europe, it is true that you will have some unfilled evenings—but that will give you a chance to wash your hair, which will probably need it by that time; and there is no rule that says you must rush around devouring every possible experience, to the point of exhaustion. If you don't agree with this, you can shower, dress, and go out to the ballet, the opera, or to a movie that will help you learn the language.

So, yes: *On whose arm will you be?* Obviously, some of the time, nobody's—which is why you may be enjoying that ballet alone, or washing your hair. What's wrong with that? Presumably you are a whole person, an adult, able occasionally to enjoy the treats of the world by yourself. Yes, you will meet people, and some of them will be men and even possible lovers—barriers are more likely to drop when you're traveling and vacationing. But to travel anywhere, as many women still do, with a feeling that your enjoyment, that the "success" of a trip depends on meeting men, is antediluvian, old-fashioned, and wasteful. It only creates anxiety and destroys your pleasure in new experiences and the marvels of the world.

As for meeting people in general, whom you meet depends partly on how you travel, and of course there are hundreds of ways to travel, from aboard freighters with twelve passengers to aboard cruise ships with hundreds of people, to Caribbean island-hopping by plane to riding in boats down the Amazon in South America—not to mention the places in which you might stop, like expensive city hotels or inexpensive pensions, and de-luxe resort hotels with a view of the beach, and the ones with no view and a bathroom for every five rooms. But you can depend on it that if you use reasonably good sense in planning your trip, and are reasonably friendly, you'll meet people.

But if you'd rather not take a chance on meeting people, you can always play it safe. Maybe you simply want to travel—want to see, perhaps, the Taj Mahal by moonlight, go to the bullfights in Madrid, visit the Colosseum in Rome, but you feel insecure about doing it on your own. If the black cloud of loneliness looms too big in your eye, you may as well be honest with yourself. Admit it, and go on a regular escorted tour.

Maybe your friends sneer at escorted tours, and perhaps you think it is too square to take one. But it is better to be square and go traveling, than to be superior and stay home. There are hundreds of escorted tours. Which one you take depends on how far your money will take you, and on whether you'd rather shop in the bazaars of Istanbul or ride in a sampan in Hong Kong. But you're always sure of seeing the night life of foreign countries and dining with other people, since your evenings are planned. And you're sure of companionship when you want it—and when you don't, you can simply duck out of a planned meal or sightseeing trip and go off exploring and meeting people on your own. You'll likely be traveling with fifteen to thirty people, so there will probably be at least one person with whom you can strike up a friendship and with whom you can go off on shopping trips or enjoy café-sitting. A Chicago fashion stylist who works terrifically hard all year insists that she would rather take an escorted trip than any other, that she hates "the mechanics of traveling, schedules and all that," and that besides, she's too knocked out by her job to cope. She turns up at New York's International Airport with her baggage, and from then on she abandons all her worries to the escort. Apparently the solution is good for her, since she returns home looking bright-eyed and rested. Since you don't have to concentrate on your baggage or tipping or checking into hotels or worrying about timetables (that's the escort's job), there's no reason not to return bright-eyed. Cleopatra probably traveled this trouble-free on her barge. And since you pay in advance for the whole works —hotels, meals, transportation, and sight-seeing trips,—you know exactly what you're spending. If this strikes you as the kind of travel you want, at least for a first-time trip, then look over lots of folders and brochures (some of them are thick as catalogues) that you can pick up at airlines offices and travel agencies; and send for even more that you see advertised in the Sunday travel section of your local newspapers. Then pick a trip that doesn't rush you through too many countries. And try to afford a medium-priced tour; rock-bottom priced tours might cut corners, and you want to assure yourself of hotels that are comfortable or at least have some charm. Naturally, on an escorted tour you won't get as much flavor of the countryside as if you were traveling on your own. And you'll meet more fellow Americans than native Europeans or South Americans or Afrikaners. But you have to make some sacrifice. And at least you are more likely to see some of those fellow Americans when you get home again to your city, where Afrikaners and South Americans may seldom turn up.

Or you might be more charmed at the idea of traveling in foreign countries with people who share an interest of yours. If so, pick a special interest trip and go on it. Gastronomy, flowers, art —there are all kinds. If one of your passions is archaeology, go off on a "dig" with other enthusiasts, digging for potsherds and such in Crete or Greece or Asia Minor. Naturally, between digging, you drink the native wines, dance the native dances, and see some of the country. If you can afford it, all you have to do to join a group is tell a travel agent, and he'll arrange it. Or you can even write a tour company directly if you see an ad you like. The best of archaeological tours is considered Swan Tours, and you join the trip in London; your companions will be English, French, Swiss, or whoever else archaeological buffs are. To go on some digs you don't even have to know an artifact from a glass of Greek retsina wine. A rather shy nurse, whom I occasionally meet in my neighborhood coffee shop, last summer had a travel agent book her on an archaeological trip to Africa and went off with a dozen archaeologists, sleeping in lodges and tents, dining, digging (she lost six pounds) having a fine time and making some good friends. Was she that interested in archaeology? "No, but I am *now*," she told me. "I just didn't want to go on a vacation to Europe or somewhere by myself—I was afriad I might not meet anybody."

And neither do you have to know a purple finch from a grackle if you want to go on a bird-watching trip through Europe's countryside with other bird-watchers, led by such knowledgeable guides as Dr. Carl Buchheister, former president of the National Audubon Society. And ecology. Ecology trips are sprouting like bean sprouts in a windowbox. The trips are getting more and more exotic: You can go on a wild-life tour in India with a group of people. Or a famous conservationist will lead you through the Danube and Rhone areas in Europe. You can go to Madagascar with a professional naturalist if you want to see the incredible birds and flowers for which Madagascar is known. Or choose something else.

Some people are snobbish about going on convention trips, but conventions are inexpensive, and tax-deductible besides. If you get a chance, go. On conventions, you generally know a few people to start with, and it's nice to go shopping or exploring with another person or two. The first year I belonged to the prestigious Fashion Group we had a convention in Tokyo, and fashion editors and assistant fashion editors, and shoe editors, and all kinds of editors who otherwise would not likely have got to Japan to see the Kabuki theater or stroll the Ginza or visit the temples of Kyoto, had fine times. I can even think of three who later saved their money and returned again to Japan.

Then there is traveling with a woman friend, if you have one available for traveling. This can be very pleasant if you handle it right, and dreadful if you don't. There is nothing I can tell you that you don't already know about the horrors of spending even two days, close as Siamese twins, with someone of possibly dissimilar tastes. If you like a cocktail before dinner, it is a dreary business indeed to sip it under the bleak eye of a nondrinker; and having a glass of wine with the meat course can make you feel like a reveler in Fellini's *Satyricon*. Or it can be something quite different (or a dozen things): "I was frustrated the whole time," a woman tells me, having just returned from a trip to Spain and Portugal with a perfectly nice, intelligent, lively, and humorous friend whose only fault was that she had spent her last cent on her fare and basic expenses, and hadn't left herself a penny for shopping pleasure, a decent dinner, a taxi, or a bullfight ticket on the shady side. This condemned her traveling companion, who likes to travel comfortably and prefers silk to muslin, to pay the bills for both their pleasures, or else travel like a Spartan. So you had better know more about your traveling companion beforehand than Freud knew about Miss O. If you are compatible and both relatively independent-minded, traveling with a friend can work beautifully. It works best when you occasionally go off on your own, pursuing your own tastes and meeting people. It is astonishing how many of the men you meet separately (or even together) will turn out to have a man friend who would be delighted to make it a foursome. And if not, presumably you're independent enough to make it firmly a twosome with a man you like well enough. I ought to say here, though, that men you meet when traveling don't necessarily have to be viewed only as romance-in-the-bud, or as sexual objects. They can be friends and delightful companions, and three people can usually lunch at a Swiss mountain inn or have dinner at a hotel with as much laughter and enjoyment as two people, and usually with a lot more.

It is also cheaper to travel with a friend, since you save money by having a double room. As for saving money in general, one way is to buy a low-priced package trip and go off to Paris-and-Amsterdam, or to Rome or Casablanca, with a package that offers you hotels and some meals, and a few "extras" like tickets for a concert or opera, and a variety of other delectables. Airlines pop up all the time like Jack-in-the-boxes with so many shiny new packages (which they dream up with tour companies) that one or another is bound to please you. Watch the newspapers for one that does, or riffle through brochures and catalogues. You can drop in at a travel agency or airline office and buy a package trip as easily as you buy a toothbrush in a drugstore. It takes all of a few minutes if you know in advance what you want—unless you go at lunch time, in which case waiting your turn can take an hour. Actually, you don't have to stir outside your office or apartment at all. A woman friend of mine who lives in a small town in Massachusetts, where the population is about fifteen hundred and there isn't even a travel agency in town, sends for dozens of brochures and studies them. When she makes up her mind, she telephones in her choice to a Boston travel agency, and they mail her everything: airline tickets, vouchers for the car she usually wants to pick up in Madrid or Cannes or Dublin, more vouchers for sightseeing trips, hotels, meals, or whatever else is included in her package. Of course, you can do this if you live in a big city, too.

It is no crime to appear naïve about travel if you've never traveled, but I know a few dozen people who would rather swim the Atlantic than ask how to get across. If that describes you, you'll feel better to learn that travel agents are used to people coming in and saying in despair, "It's snowing, get me out of here—Where is it warm?" Or "I've been saving up for two years and I have three weeks' vacation—Where should I go?" Airlines' reservations clerks can help you too; they will happily suggest one or another of their tours for you, and can even give you information and help on hotels and car rentals, and so on.

But above all, don't be shy about using a travel agent. You ought to see *everything* in the store before you buy, and the agent *has* everything. One of the priceless things he has is professional know-how (that will eventually save you money). And since he represents *all* the airlines, and the steamship companies and big tour companies (and little ones), he can send you to Morocco or England or Hungary or Israel, packaged or unpackaged. He knows about pony-trekking in Ireland and wine tours in France and flower trips in England. If you want to go on an African safari complete with white hunter, he can arrange it, or if you want to recover from your exhausting job by staying at a quiet (and inexpensive) hotel by Lake Lucerne, he can arrange that. And when he doesn't know something, he knows where to look it up instantly.

And don't worry that you're not being at all helpful to him, about where you want to go, if you don't know. You can expect him to make suggestions that are sometimes inspired, and to work out a trip that fits the amount of money you want to spend. He can also give you information about getting your passport, tell you what vaccinations you do or don't need, reserve your plane seats, provide your tickets, reserve your hotel rooms, make your train or plane connections. He can advise you on sightseeing and arrange it for you, rent a car abroad for you. If you're thinking it would be fun to travel on some of those glide-like-silk trains in Europe, where they feed you delicious meals, ask him lots of questions about it, and have him explain all the different classes and kinds —he'll know. He can tell you about an eight-day bicycle race in Italy and get tickets for you at the Edinburgh Music Festival. Or he can book you on wonderful motorcoach tours if that's what interests you (and can tell you about dozens more). Ask him anything, like what the weather is in Geneva in April and how to pack. If you favor a cruise, have him tell you everything he can, which is plenty, what with his Official Steamship Guide, which includes 230 shipping lines, and their "this year's" new cruises, with their bewildering schedules of departure dates, countries they visit, and so on.

If you think you see your money dwindling away, what with all this service, you should know the facts about travel agencies. Naturally the agent gets paid for all this, but luckily *you* do not generally do the paying. He gets paid standard commissions by the airlines and hotels and other companies whose services he sells. That means that you pay the same price for an airline ticket whether you stand in line at an airline office or whether you buy it from the travel agent, since the airline pays him a commission. If you buy a package trip, you pay nothing extra to him; he gets his commission from the packager (which is the airline and a tour company). If he books you into a resort hotel and most other hotels, there's no charge either, since the hotels pay his commission. Same for steamship reservations if you're going on a cruise; *they* pay him, not you. If you have him rent a car abroad for you, the car company pays him the commission, not you. And it's the same with group escorted tours and any other prearranged tours; *they* pay him, not you.

Naturally, though, it is hardly fair to ask a travel agent to do everything but vaccinate you, when you're taking only an eight-day, three-hundred-dollar trip to the Algarve. And he will think so, too. If you want him to help you rent a rowboat or take care of supplying you with foreign money (to tip porters the moment you set foot on foreign soil), and perform a dozen other such services that take his time and don't pay him commissions, you'll likely have to pay a small fee. Unless your trip is sizable enough to pay him reasonably satisfactory commissions, he'll certainly have to charge a fee for making extra transatlantic telephone calls or sending cables to make any special arrangements you might fancy. And of course if you want an entire luxury itinerary worked out just for you, with a chauffeur-driven car meeting you at 2:00 A.M. at the Nice airport, you have to pay a fee for such professional service —just the same as if you're having a dress custom-made instead of buying it off the rack at Bloomingdale's.

I am assuming that once you begin to travel, you will become infatuated with it. So you had better pick a good travel agent in the beginning; it may turn into a long friendship. There are supposed to be ways to tell a good agent from a bad or indifferent, or even a fly-by-night one. My advice, after my years as a travel writer and editor, and having also been part-owner of a prize-winning travel agency (of which my husband was vice president) is to go to an agent that has been solidly in business for plenty of years, so you'll know he's not a fly-by-night. It helps if he's a member of ASTA, which is the American Society of Travel Agents. You'll know whether he is or not because you'll see the ASTA oval insignia in his window. It means he meets certain national standards.

And of course you want an agent who is *sympatico*. You will know very soon whether he (or she) is or is not *sympatico,* because the *sympatico* one will be on the same mental wave-length as you, and not a thousand miles off it. A friend of mine, who is a dreamy and tasteful and well-to-do career woman in Buffalo, once told a travel agent to whom she had gone for the first time, that she hoped to stay "in a quaint little mountain hotel or two, in Switzerland," to which the agent superiorly replied, "They are too provincial, and not for you—you need something modern." And while he was still leafing through a thick book of hotels for something "modern," my dreamy friend quietly disappeared out the door.

The more adventurous you are, the more bare-boned arrangements you ought to make, so you can do more exploring on your own or with a friend. You can make up your own itinerary and have a travel agent book it for you, or you can even book a bone-simple trip yourself. But unless you are a mathematical wizard or you'd like to spend your evenings corresponding with hotel-keepers in Tunisia or Romania, and figuring out train schedules and kilometers, don't book anything too complicated or you're likely to discover it is hardly worth it—much like a friend of mine who built a house without a contractor; it cost her head-cracking figuring and lots of warfare with plumbers, electricians and carpenters, all without a cent saved. And it's a wonder her house didn't come out lopsided.

But if you're going to travel with the assurance of a world traveler (and you should), you should settle down for some evenings with travel books and brochures, and gain a little travel expertise. It is always more pleasurable, and even a little heady, to be in the know. You should possess a certain sophisticated knowledge, no matter who books your trip. And it saves you money if, before you plan what country or countries to visit, you know that, for instance, it costs about twenty dollars a day to travel medium class in France, but that it costs hardly ten dollars in Austria. And that Yugoslavia costs about $7.50 a day—but Italy will cost you double that. That Spain is cheap. And England expensive. And that if you're in Zurich or Milan or some other foreign cities and want to rent a car, some car companies are affiliated with Hertz or Avis or National, so if you have your credit card with you, you won't have to leave a deposit. And it is only smart to know all about excursion air fares and economy fares, and free stopovers, and ship-travel discounts, and Eurailpass and British Rail savings, and so on.

The more you know, the freer you'll feel to go off on your own, completely alone, exploring, meeting people, picking up a smattering of this or that language, maybe even finding time for a bit of solitude and reflection. It is no accident that through history so many poets, painters and writers who traveled alone in foreign countries became enamored of the lake country in Italy, a mountain town in Spain, or a provincial fishing village on France's southern coast, so that the place turns up again and again in their work—a recurring theme like a song that stays with them forever. That kind of stamp upon the mind comes when you're alone. Traveling alone is more conducive to it. Alone, you have time to think, to reflect, to *see*.

And alone, with no one but you to take care of tipping and baggage and train schedules, you gradually gain a certain aplomb, a delicious feeling of becoming adept and competent in a foreign country. When one day in Zurich a Swiss woman asked me the way to the Zum Storchen Hotel and I was able to give her exact directions in gestures and basic German, I felt more at home, possibly, than that native-born Swiss. A few incidents like this, and forever after you have self-confidence and a certain independence and *savoir-faire* as you step off a plane in Athens, Caracas, Nice. You are breathing different air. You are breathing the intoxicating air of the continental traveler.

When you travel completely alone, you also have the luxury of privacy, but when you want to be with people you can be: You simply pick up a couple of days' tour wherever you are. There are dozens of these everywhere. In Copenhagen, for instance, join a day's motorcoach tour and go off to visit Hamlet's castle at Elsinore . . . or take a whole-day tour from Copenhagen to Sweden by bus and ferry, all for six dollars . . . or try a half-dozen other tours. Ask the desk clerk at your hotel what's available and good; he may even be able to book it for you. Or you can just stop in at any little travel agency near your hotel and choose from the array of trips. A motorcoach crowd is always congenial. In France, join a two-day motorcoach trip to the chateau country, for instance. Once, in Turkey, when I felt a sudden desire to be with people, I joined a three-day motorcoach tour, and with a small group of people traveled from Istanbul to Ephesus, stopping overnight at a small hotel in Chanakale on the seacoast, and again at Izmir. We lunched and dined together, and in Troy and Ephesus explored the famous ruins with a guide. It was just enough socializing to put me in touch. Salutary and sufficient. My aim wasn't to form undying friendships, but to relax with people.

Or a half-day tour for companionship is sometimes all you want, or even all you have time for. Or a day. What you can do in a day is staggering. A couple of years ago, I arrived in Edinburgh late one night, had only the following day to spend there, and didn't feel like spending it alone. So the next morning, at 9:30, I went off on an all-day motorcoach tour of Scotland's western highlands. Everyone else on the trip was Scottish—vacationing Scotsmen out to see Stirling Castle and the moors of Rob Roy, and Loch Lomond, and Loch Katrine, where we stopped for lunch at a lakeside hotel. Late in the afternoon we stopped again in a small village, and in an upstairs tea shop had tea and scones and butter and jam, all of us sitting at tables for six, and all very friendly by this time. At 8:00 o'clock that night we drove past the Firth of Forth and back into Edinburgh. One day, but an unforgettable one. The trip cost four dollars, not counting my lunch. Someone else insisted on paying for my tea.

But if you want to meet people first thing, go on a few days' tour the minute you arrive. Pick one that's close to your heart, that really appeals to you. A city-bound acquaintance of mine did this with particular success last year, when she went off to England on a three-week vacation. She loves boats and was in a sylvan mood, so instead of spending her first days in London, she booked her first week on one of the canal boats that go lazing through the winding inland rivers of England. She made friends with the other eight or ten people aboard, meeting two or three whom she could see later in London. Not only that, but this city-fatigued careerist (she works for an industrial engineer) after a week of fresh air was tanned, rested, and (she insists) looked like a blossoming tearose. She had a wonderful time in London, and no wonder. If you're so minded, you can try something similar (or even the same thing; a week on a canal boat in England costs about ninety dollars, including meals). Ask a travel agent about it—or if riverboating in France intrigues you more, ask about the six-day riverboat trips that are becoming popular in France (but they cost more).

When you travel alone, it's easier to meet people when you travel off the beaten path. A couple or a man who wouldn't look twice at you if you're having dinner alone at the Savoy in London, will be intrigued if they see you in East Africa, dining alone in a Nairobi hotel. And under such circumstances you're likely to be friendly yourself, more approachable, and a tinge of loneliness might make you more interested in meeting them. If it doesn't, and you want to decline their attentions, in Nairobi or elsewhere, that's up to you; but it's at least nice to have a choice.

If you are going to meet natives of other countries—Spaniards in Spain, Yugoslavians in Yugoslavia, Romanians in Romania, and so on, you will have to be a little enterprising. An amazing number of Europeans speak English, so becoming friendly won't be as difficult as you might think. The idea is to look up, say, in Paris, Parisians who share your profession or sport or hobby. Your job may be the best door-opener. Once, when I was working on a Hearst magazine, I arrived in Paris for a four-day stay, and hadn't been in my hotel room ten minutes before I telephoned the Paris office of *Harper's Bazaar* and made an appointment to see a fellow editor who was a Frenchwoman I'd never met. The next morning, I met her at the *Bazaar* offices for a chat; it was the end of August, and the fashion collections were just over, and models and most editors had fled Paris after the showings. Except for the editor I saw, only an art director still remained. He took me to lunch at a small nearby bistro where we ate *sole amandine,* drank a light wine and had a pleasant time discussing the magazine business and a dozen other subjects. He also gave me the names of three or four Paris photographers I might be able to use in future work, and I called them, and made several appointments. By the time I left Paris four days later I had made some business friends, got a more inside view of the current Paris activities, from *boîtes* to politics, and had found two photographers I could use later on.

Wrack your brains for your particular *entrée,* and go to it. On a plane returning from Caracas I once met a woman hotel-banquet manager who'd had a marvelous time visiting hotels and dropping in on fellow hotel-banquet managers in South America. And I can think of a woman who works behind the scenes of a TV quiz show, and who always checks around her office before she goes on a pleasure trip. "Does anybody here know anybody who works on a quiz show in Rome?" she will ask, if she's going to Rome. Or Casablanca, if she's going to Casablanca. She once even wrote to a broadcasting station in a small city she wanted to visit outside of Rio de Janeiro, and actually found two people who were enchanted to meet a woman from a big, "sophisticated" TV quiz show (theirs was a radio quiz show). She took them to lunch and they took her to the local nightclub.

If any traveling foreigners have ever visited you in your own home city, visit them back. Once, in New York, I received a telephone call from an Israeli newspaperwoman, who introduced herself and said she was curious to see how an American magazine worked. I invited her to my editorial office, showed her through the departments, introduced her to various editors, and took her to lunch, where she then told me all about how her newspaper was run in Israel. And when next I visit that country, I'll visit that editor and her newspaper.

Assuming you've also had the foresight to fill a notebook with names of friends' friends drummed up here and there before you leave home, you should be able to meet enough people. But if not, a foreign country's "Meet the People" program might suit you. I know people who would flee from such an idea in embarrassment, and it may be just the kind of thing you want to avoid. Nevertheless, I know a fairly sophisticated American photographer (in this case a male) who works a lot in Europe and has become fast friends with a Swiss family he met that way and which he now sees fairly regularly. If you want to arrange to meet the Swiss, Irish, Norwegians, Japanese, and so on, let their nearest tourist bureau in the United States know something about you by letter (get their address from your nearest friendly travel agency or else from that country's nearest airline office . . . or even look up the New York office address at your local library in their copy of the Manhattan Yellow Pages, which most libraries have). The tourist bureau will see what compatible people they can match you up with. You have to do this, usually, before you leave home, and when you get to Ireland or wherever, that branch of the tourist bureau takes over. In fact, when you're in a foreign city and you feel in the dark about how to get in touch with the local bridge club or fellow dieticians (if you're a dietician), or the horticultural society, or whatever, the tourist bureau often can help. Sometimes they even have surprising information. Once, on my way home from Europe, I arrived in Copenhagen late in the afternoon and with no plane until the following morning. So there I was in a hotel room at the Royal Hotel, with no plans and knowing no one. Taking a chance, I telephoned the Danish tourist bureau and asked if there were any other press people in town. Yes, they told me, a Paris travel writer who wrote considerably for an American paper was in Copenhagen and he too was staying at the Royal. I called him, introduced myself, and mentioned a couple of mutual friends. He was delighted; he too had just arrived and hadn't yet made any plans. We met for a drink, went to Oskar Davidsen's for some of their famous Danish open-faced sandwiches for dinner, then went on to complete my companion's newspaper assignment: exploring Copenhagen night life.

Even meeting people, you are likely in for a touch of nose-pressed-to-windowpane wistfulness when it comes to glamorous foreign-city night life—if you like nightclubs, that is. You can't count on an escort for nightclubbing; it is simply a matter of luck, in whom you meet; and it isn't very smart to compromise by accepting an invitation from the kind of man you'd avoid at home, just for the sake of an evening of glamorous night life. Considering all the benefits of traveling alone, though, missing a few nightclubs isn't such a bad price to pay. But if you're bent on getting a glimpse of night life and haven't an escort, you can always go on one of the night-life tours in Venice, London, Monte Carlo, and a dozen other cities: You go with a group of couples and other single people, but the tours are not romantic, and you are liable to feel more like a sociologist viewing the strange native tribal customs than like a romantic character in a French movie. You may think you are far too sophisticated for such a tour, which well could be, since most of us are. But it won't be the only compromise you're making in life. And the cost is reasonable (between ten and twenty dollars), considering the entertainment, the food, and drinks. And at least every one of the tours has something worthwhile. If you bear with the early part of the better Paris tour, which is "touristy," you will at least finally reach the Lido, with its spectacular and beautiful show, and where you will drink champagne. A night-life tour in Athens takes you on a drive to the

Acropolis, you drink wine at a *taverna,* and have dinner at a typical Greek night club—all for ten dollars. In Istanbul, you pay ten dollars, which includes two drinks and the show at one of the best nightclubs, or at the sophisticated Hilton Roof, where they always have an exquisite belly dancer.

I have been talking mainly about Europe, in the interests of simplicity, but most of what I have been really talking about all along is a philosophy in traveling alone. It applies whether you visit the tropical lushness and brilliance of Haiti or take a five-day cruise to the Caribbean, or even take a trip from Denver to explore New Orleans (which is certainly foreign if you are from Denver). In essence, I am talking about a new kind of woman traveler who goes where she pleases and does as she pleases, at least insofar as her budget will allow. In the process she gains aesthetic pleasures, the viewpoint of a cosmopolite, and a certain confidence and glamour besides. These are live-alone assets not to be ignored.

If you are thinking again about your budget, as you should, I might mention that the woman I know who travels most successfully is not rich or even particularly well off. And she doesn't afford her trips by traveling hippie-style, staying at hostels with youngsters and packing along a knapsack, which is fine for kids but incongruous and ridiculous for an adult. She is, in fact, the manager of a Boston bookstore, and when I first met her about eight years ago she was a rather unworldly book clerk who hadn't been much farther than Rutland, Vermont. Her first trip was the year after I met her, when she was twenty-six, and it was to recover from a short-lived and disastrous marriage, and an uncle paid for half of it. It was the cheapest out-of-season excursion night flight to Puerto Rico, and she stayed in a third-rate hotel in the old part of San Juan and slept under a mosquito net. But when she got back to Boston she began to spend her lunch hours reading all the travel books in the bookstore's stock, plus any number of travel and airlines and railroad brochures. Since then she has learned how to travel almost anywhere inexpensively. She has a yearly three-week vacation and she takes an extra week, and she has now been to India and the British Isles, and she has gone to

Alexandria, a city that lured her after she read Lawrence Durrell's *Justine*. She has visited most of the middle European countries by comfortable but inexpensive trains, and she has stayed at fairy-tale old castles like the Matzleinsdorf in Austria where meals with a room cost about five dollars a day, and in Portugal she has stayed in *posadas,* which are charming inns that cost about four dollars a night including good meals with wine. If you woke her up out of a deep sleep in the middle of the night, she could probably tell you without an instant's hesitation the right season to be in Spain so as not to miss the bullfights, and when to avoid the festival in this or that city (she hates crowds), and what small *pensions* in a dozen countries are friendly, inexpensive, and delightful. It all seems to have done her a lot of good. The bookshop customers look on her as "something rich and strange" and will buy almost anything she recommends, and I have heard that a travel agent has twice proposed to her (and was turned down), but not because of her flair for travel.

CHAPTER 11

Private and Personal

One of the biggest hazards of living alone is the temptation to be profligate of your time: to give it away. In fact, I know some live-aloners who hand out their precious hours as though they were penny candy. And anybody who asks, gets some.

And people do ask. You have probably noticed that when you live alone, an amazing number of people assume that *your* time is *their* time. In between the times they leave you as solidly alone as a lighthouse keeper, they are liable to telephone and ask if you'd mind doing all sorts of things, such as entertaining out-of-town cousins, or putting up vacationing friends on a cot in your living room. *There you are all alone, with a whole apartment to yourself, aren't you?* is the ingenuous implication that comes humming over the telephone line. Or you may have acquaintances who ask you to take up charity collections or beat the drums for their political candidate. Or address five hundred letters for a cause they've given their hearts to.

If you are at all susceptible to such invasions of your time, you ought to stiffen up. You will need to scotch the notion that you are on call. You will have to make clear to people that *My time is NOT your time.*

The reason I say you will have to do this is that your time is valuable. Regardless of whether you think you have too much time alone or not, *valuing your time is important*. It is *your* time. It is precious time. How you spend it on any particular evening is your own affair; it is perfectly legitimate to tell people you're busy if you'd rather read the newspaper, take a bath, do exercises in a leotard, or even do nothing. And you don't have to feel guilty if you refuse to head an anti-pollution campaign or put up a cousin's best friend as a weekend house guest. Guilt, in such cases, is out (it went out with lame ducks).

It is not selfish, it is *realistic* to value your time. If I am leaning rather heavily on this point, one reason is that if you don't value your time, you will make dates you regret, feed dinner to people you dislike, and suffer the ennui of polite and tedious conversation with mere acquaintances. You might even be doing these things when you could be enjoying a solitary private concert (on hi-fi) with a glass of wine, or taking a needed nap. Doing any of those socially polite things, in any case, leads to a general feeling of hostility, a subterranean awareness of waste, and is bad for the digestion besides. I am not being facetious about this, but factual. There is no good reason, since the decision is all yours and not partly a marital partner's or anyone else's, not to decide to do only what pleases you.

But another reason I am so insistent on being parsimonious with your time is that few things are more important than the time you have for yourself. I am talking now about the value of solitude, the pleasures of solitude and reflection, and having time for projects of your own. Solitude is a kind of manna, one of the blessings of living alone. You need solitude to renew yourself, like dipping yourself into a refreshing spring, and you need it not in bits and pieces, but in sizable chunks of evenings. And you should have it when *you* want it—not as leftovers after other people's whims or demands. You're first; they're second. An advertising copywriter friend of mine recognizes this, with particular success: She goes out on dates twice a week with a particular man, and she may or may not go out two other evenings—but she defends with the ferocity of a tiger her right to preserve those three other evenings for a project of her own, something to do with a reading plan that a casual encounter with William James's *Varieties of Religious Experience* launched her on well over a year ago. Her apartment has become, to her, what her male friend jokingly but admiringly calls "a palace of becoming"—and this is actually a pretty clever comment, since she is becoming quite a person. She has discovered a subject that fascinates her, and she is insisting on the time and solitude to pursue it. As far as she is concerned, a three-hour span of time alone on those evenings is equivalent to a handful of rubies; it is far from just empty "give-away" time.

What we are pushing here is the value of *sophisticated aloneness:* the ability to spend evenings home alone and use them enjoyably to grow. But you will have to be stubbornly selfish about it, or rather, what other people think is selfish. But it is not really selfish, for of course you will never do anybody else any good unless you do yourself some good in the first place.

Spending specific evenings at home and enjoying it is not quite as simple as cooking an egg. It is, even, an art. The best plan is to find an interest or project and plan to devote, say, Monday, Wednesday, and Thursday evenings to it, no matter what—keeping those evenings as inviolate as though you'd pulled up a drawbridge. You'll need solid blocks of time. Arnold Bennett, the shrewd and famous turn-of-the-century writer once even wrote a whole book on the pleasures of spending solid blocks of one's evening hours alone, exploring a particular subject. His advice was, in essence, not to try to swallow the whole world, but to choose, for instance, a limited period in history, or a limited subject. Or perhaps a single author. Mr. Bennett suggested that the best way to explore a subject so that you'll get the most gratification out of it is to do it without rushing. In his words: "Forget the goal; think only of the surrounding country; and after a period, perhaps when you least expect it, you will suddenly find yourself in a lovely town on a hill."

In a lovely town on a hill. Really, when you live alone, there can be lovely towns on hills. It only remains to find them. Knowing all about Greek mythology or the great wine vineyards of France, or the elaborate costumes of the T'ang Dynasty priests—it doesn't matter. If you had a high school interest in medieval heraldry, or a curiosity about how *really* to listen to symphony music appreciatively, revive it. Explore it, treat it well. After all, there are plenty of evenings when you're going to be alone anyway, by choice or not. And what better way to spend them than deeply involved in some subject that gives you pleasure, whether learning all about oriental herbs or modern architecture? Or even if you have some minor talent that's dormant, like playing the bass fiddle, revive it, too, and treat it well—not, as someone once said of a writer who was wasting his ability, "treating it like a crazy old woman with a diamond." It all makes for marvelous relaxation besides, a fact that most productive people discover: for Einstein it was playing the violin and listening to Bach; for Nabokov, it is studying butterflies. Live-alone actress Sylvia Sydney became so fascinated by her needlepoint that she wrote a book about it and now designs patterns and sells her needlepoint kits nationally, in department stores and by mail order, and runs the whole project from her country home in New England. As for that, even if you don't plan to make a dime at it, and it is not at all your main "limited subject," using your hands creatively—matting pictures, gilding a picture frame, antiquing furniture—is anyway marvelously satisfying. Psychologists talk lately about how desirable manual activity is for all human beings, that, for one thing, it stimulates you and starts you being more creative in other ways too. One psychologist calls it "a conquest of love over hate, of the creative instinct over the destructive or self-destructive drive"—which we all have plenty of. Almost anything useful or good that you can do with your hands vanquishes self-destructive impulses like brooding-and-drinking or chain-smoking. Whether you call it "creative action" as some psychologists do, or whether you call it crocheting, it is relaxing, fun, and good for you.

If a consuming interest starts to take over your life, it will generally create a more fascinating one, live-alone or not. I am thinking at the moment of Helen MacInnes who started by keeping little journals, for herself alone, on her particular interest, which was international affairs and what she calls "grand politics." Finally one day she reached the point where she wanted something more than her daily life provided. So she began to write *Above Suspicion,* her first novel of international suspense. She then just kept on writing without even waiting to see how *Above Suspicion* would be received. So far, she has written something like fourteen best sellers in a row.

You might even cleverly spend your specific evenings on an interest that will give you a jump on the future. One friend of mine, who works in Washington, D.C., in a government job, is now forty-nine. In six years she is entitled to retire at half-pay. She is a woman who likes to live charmingly and even extravagantly, which she will not be able to do in Washington at half-salary, but which she very well feels she can do in a small town just outside of a particular European city. And she ought to know, since she has read and studied countless publications in search of her kind of place—her kind of place involving warm weather, flowers, and cultural activities not too far away. In line with her plan, she spends certain evenings at home studying the language (on records), and the culture of this fascinating (to her) country. She is also learning how to teach, via a correspondence course, since she hopes to tutor a few pupils in English. She has already spent a couple of vacations in the town of her choice, and has made two or three good friends there; one is an American couple, the husband a commuter to the nearby city where he works for an American company. She also subscribes to the town's local newspaper and reads it (with difficulty). Of course her plans may change (lately it looks as though she is liable to marry), but the entire project is anyway an enormous pleasure to her.

If you are this busy, you are bound to offend some of your friends, at least at first. For one thing, if you have friends with a habit of dropping in, you'll have to suggest delicately (or strongly) that they telephone first. You will have to convey to your family in Seattle or wherever that you are not a way-station with a collapsible cot in the closet. You will have to learn to say on the telephone that you're busy right now and can you call them back another time. At least you will have to do these things if you expect to have any of those chunks of evening time for yourself. I can't imagine Nabokov letting anyone interfere with the time he wants to spend on butterflies; the thought of my knocking on his door at such a time and seeing it slowly swing open freezes me with terror.

You won't lose your friends, anyway, by laying down rules. They'll only decide you're more worthwhile, desirable, admirable, and enviable. You're demanding consideration, and everyone respects people who do.

Demanding consideration, *making demands,* is vital. You should, you *must* insist on top-drawer consideration. It establishes you as a person with a healthy and dearly beloved ego. Too many live-aloners are shy about this. "Oh, never mind, I'll pick it up," a friend of mine limply tells the cleaner, instead of insisting he deliver the cleaning he promised her. And "The motor was knocking again even before I got home from the garage," she will tell me woefully of her recently fixed car, "but I just didn't have the nerve to go back." She is a divorcée who feels nervously vulnerable without the familiar "security" of a husband to back her up. When she orders sirloin, and chuck arrives, she doesn't murmur. If the liquor store delivers the wrong wine, she only sighs, instead of demanding the right one. Alone, she is afraid to make demands on anyone—friends, acquaintances, shopkeepers. Alone, she prefers, as she says, "not to complain." Hers is a poor-little-orphan complex that no live-aloner can afford. If you're in this fix, complain. Complain! *Do* complain! We insist on it. It is not only vital to your self-esteem, but it clears the air and you get the job done—

whatever it is—correctly. Complain at the hairdresser if you have to wait too long under the drier, complain if the hairstyle isn't what you clearly asked for, complain if a friend is late for a date. Get mad where it counts (it counts wherever the situation demands it). Insist when you should insist. Insist without qualm and without quarter. A little iron in your character is something you needn't be afraid of showing. The most feminine live-alone women insist on knowing who they are, and they invariably demand what they should demand, whether their name is Jane Smith or Ava Gardner.

And of course, as Theodor Reik remarked, "To express unafraid and unashamed what one really thinks and feels is one of the great consolations of life." It is indeed. It also helps remarkably to get over occasional feelings of depression that are often brought on by letting people walk all over you, when you are perfectly aware that you shouldn't. It is amazing how often you can discover that a moody depression is due to nothing more than going against your own standards of how you *ought* to act, and consequently feeling rotten about it and getting depressed. While I am quoting I might again quote the redoubtable Arnold Bennett, whose analogy on this subject charms us: "I care not what your principles are. Your principles may induce you to believe in the righteousness of burglary. I don't mind. All I urge is that a life in which conduct does not fairly well accord with principles is a silly life; and that conduct can only be made to accord with principles by means of daily examination, reflection, and resolution. What leads to the permanent sorrowfulness of burglars is that their principles are contrary to burglary. If they genuinely believed in the moral excellence of burglary, penal servitude would simply mean so many happy years for them; all martyrs are happy, because their conduct and their principles agree." Of course, if your principles are that you should let people walk all over you, there isn't anything more we can suggest.

As for getting moody and depressed in general, live-aloners can get just as depressed as people who don't live alone. Getting depressed now and then isn't any more common to live-aloners than anyone else, as a quick glance at your various married friends (or a confidential chat with some of them) will tell you. Depression doesn't come from living alone any more than the common cold comes from eating beef stew. It comes, as you are undoubtedly aware, from a variety of causes, some deeply psychical, and some as simple as a love affair gone sour. Depression is like hunger—everybody has it. Like ships have barnacles, people have depressions. You can't escape occasional depression, since it is as essential as our other emotions; so the most sensible thing to do is recognize that everybody needs a little depression, and is anyway going to have a little—but that you can nevertheless "contain" it.

I am not, by the way, talking about the sort of deep depression that both live-aloners and other people can suffer from, and for which the obvious answer is a trip to the psychoanalyst. Or maybe you have other problems you feel you can't cope with alone, and for which analysis is in order. Luckily, when you live alone, the decision is all yours. No one else is involved. It is your time. It is your money. If you think analysis is where it's worth putting it, go ahead. You don't even need the excuse that you're in dire straits—that you suspect yourself of nymphomania or are bewilderedly unhappy or are a compulsive gambler. Maybe you just want to stop smoking, or get over a neurosis that interferes with your job or your creativity, or you're afraid to go up in elevators, or have some other symptom you'd like to get rid of. It is still your money, and you can go out and buy as much help as you can afford.

There is also a popular notion abroad that loneliness goes with living alone, as bread goes with butter. Maybe that was so in the days when live-alone women were subjected to social pressures to view their single state with irremediable gloom. But other people may really have had more of a corner on the loneliness market than live-aloners—or, as Anton Chekhov in the 1800s advised, "If you are afraid of loneliness, don't marry." This Chekhovian viewpoint is a little too cynically one-sided for me, though it does, for my purposes, act as a balance wheel. I am aware, though, that some live-aloners are still so susceptible to the myth that loneliness is a concomitant of living alone, that they even work hard at it, egging it on. I know one self-absorbed widow who, after two years, still lives in a flood of tears: when her friends telephone her, they can hear her stereo in the background playing "Goodbye Happiness,

Hello Loneliness," but most of her friends, in exasperation, no longer bother to telephone.

Loneliness, just like moods of depression, is a perfectly human feeling that everyone has. You're stuck with it. But living in a state of euphoria would be bland and boring. I myself favor a touch of loneliness, like salt on my steak, rosemary on my peas. It adds a bit of flavor.

Just a touch, of course. But if you have come this far in this book, and are reasonably receptive to it, a touch is all you'll have time for.

CHAPTER 12

Solitary Dieting...
Drinking...
Eating...
Cooking

Few things can brighten a live-alone life like good meals, and we suggest that you passionately embrace this philosophy. We admire one particular woman who looks forward to March principally because it brings the season of tender green and crisp asparagus which she dines on (the hot stalks on toast, drenched with butter, sprinkled with lemon juice) with great joy. We are not suggesting you be this singleminded. Or even that you aim for the enviable pleasure of that Armenian billionaire oil tycoon, Nubar Gulbenkian, who always dined so well, and in fact enjoyed a good meal so much that he once declared that when he died he hoped to die while dining at Maxim's in Paris, and added hastily "—after the dessert, of course." We are simply mentioning the importance of food, good food, delicious food. In fact, food is so important to most people that when, in a recent controversy in the *New York Times* about white eggs versus brown eggs, British author J. B. Priestley cast a slur on Americans, saying that they learn about sex from manuals instead of in bed, ten Americans were indignant about Mr. Priestley's comments on Americans' attitude toward brown eggs, and only one picked up the slur about sex . . . which led to a London newspaperman observing that "food is a more emotive topic than sex." I seem to be getting rather deeply into another area here, but I think it only fair to go one step further and comment that the American (a woman) who was indignant about the slur, said that Americans were nevertheless one up on the British, who never seemed to learn about sex at all. I am not going to go any further in this minor war . . . though I will say that the London correspondent said that that was certainly a good joke—but no less inaccurate than the original remark.

From all this, I hope I have made my point: Few things are as important as food. This should also make it clear that if you harbor any unfortunate live-alone attitude about meals, along the lines of *Why bother, it's only me?* you should immediately cast it out. It is a feeling that leads to drearily drinking one's orange juice out of a jelly glass and eating scraps out of the refrigerator (I even know a woman who does this and who never actually has a meal—and often can't remember whether she did eat or not). It is the attitude that leads some live-aloners to decide they are "too tired" to bother, when they get home at 6:00 o'clock or 6:30 from the office. This, of course, is exactly when you should treat yourself not badly, but well. When you are tired is no time for dining on leftover limp vegetables. When you are too tired, there are better moves than "throwing something together" or shoveling in some scraps. A good meal takes the chill off anxiety and replaces exhaustion with warmth and comfort. The thing to do is hang up your coat, boil up some water, and pour yourself a cup of hot bouillon spiked with a good dash of sherry. Drink this, accompanied by a buttered English biscuit, while seated in a soft chair in the living room with your feet up. It will give you the energy to listen to the news on the radio or read a chapter in a book. It will also give you a nice glow in your stomach . . . and in due time you can relaxedly go into the kitchen and fix something simple and attractive to eat.

If it is going to be simple and attractive, you will have to have a few simple and attractive things on your kitchen shelves and in the refrigerator. A batch of things from a gourmet shop. Some things in the freezer, like frozen Italian beans and cauliflower in butter sauce. Perhaps bake-and-serve rolls, so you can pop one or two into the oven. If you really are exhausted, this is hardly the time for fancy cookery. But simple is as good as fancy, and can be elegant and delicious. A cheese omelet with baby frankfurters on toast points is a tasty evening meal. Try sautéed-in-butter kidneys and mushrooms with lemon juice, a crisp roll, a salad of bibb lettuce, followed by espresso coffee. Or chicken livers on buttered toast. A broiled hamburger that you rubbed first with garlic and salt and sprinkled with parsley is heavenly with a thin slice of bleu cheese, a glass of wine, a roll, and salad of lettuce leaves only. So is a supper of two cut-up, hot hard-boiled eggs in cheese sauce (white sauce with a dash of Worcestershire sauce and grated Cheddar) accompanied by broiled tomato halves topped with butter and basil, and with a roll and cups of hot Chinese green tea. And try broiled sardines on toast with butter and mustard, sprinkled with lemon. Any fish (fresh or frozen, for instance whiting) split, brushed with butter, parsley and salt, and baked fifteen minutes in the oven is delicate gourmet fare that's perfect with a plain boiled potato topped with yoghurt, and a can of tiny French peas (with a pinch of basil).

Where you eat this meal is in comfort and coziness, perhaps on a tray on a couch in the living room, or at a small table with a lamp on it, in your bedroom (mine is a thirty six-inch round table and instead of a lamp I have a candlestick of a tin Mexican angel, kneeling and holding up the candle), or some equally reposeful nook or corner. Never do you eat it standing in the kitchen, like a stork on one leg, or at a kitchen counter that faces the wall and has no place for your knees. For of course you are also feeding your soul. I am using the word "soul" here in the sense of all its intangibles, those intangibles that involve warmth and emotional feelings of well-being. By twilight, by lamplight, by candlelight, dining like this is one of the most civilized moments in life.

A dinner—or breakfast, or late-night snack, or any other meal, for that matter—is even more soul-satisfying when you eat it off of attractive china. Tea really does taste better out of a shell-thin Limoges cup than out of one of those greenish glass ones from the five-and-ten. And there is something richly satisfying about the clink of a real silver knife and fork on a fine china plate. I am certainly not urging you to go out and splurge on a set of china or silver. But I hope you can afford to invest in one fine china cup and saucer, perhaps Wedgwood or Royal Doulton, from your nearest secondhand shop—which in my neighborhood costs a total of $2.50 to $3.50. If you can afford more, a pretty five-piece place-setting in my neighborhood goes for about ten dollars, and you dine off it royally every evening. You probably already have at least a "good" china cup and saucer in the closet, waiting for . . . what? Use it. You probably also have a few pieces of sterling silver tucked away, and if so, use them. *Now* is the time you have been saving them for. If you haven't any, why not invest in at least one place setting of sterling? Or maybe only in an antique silver teaspoon, which in my neighborhood (and probably yours) goes for about three dollars.

It is also true that a peach peeled with a pearl-handled fruit knife tastes better than one peeled with any old table knife. Richer, juicier. A pearl-handled fruit knife will never wear out, and at those same shops costs about two to three dollars, which is a remarkably small investment for such aesthetics. As for the peach itself (which you are of course serving yourself on your real china plate), one rosy, luscious peach has it all over three inferior unripe ones. Buy your fruit, any fruit, perfect and dead-ripe, and in small quantities— such as one at a time. Buy it at the best market, and if their vegetable man doesn't love you for it (and he never will), he will at least come to tolerate you, provided you buy your potatoes and other vegetables at the same place.

Other accoutrements you might have for solitary meals are two champagne glasses: one for Sunday morning breakfasts, when it is very luxurious to fill it with orange juice over cracked ice, to drink in bed while reading the newspapers (the other glass is for when you want to celebrate something with someone one afternoon or evening, and with champagne, not orange juice).

Beyond that, you might have a pretty table mat or so . . . and perhaps a demitasse cup and saucer for when you're in the mood for concluding your dinner with a cup of espresso, preferably hot and strong, with a twist of lemon peel and a shaving of bitter chocolate. An old Venetian proverb goes: "Coffee from the top of the cup, chocolate from the bottom." I thoroughly agree, and you should try it.

As for breakfasts, deciding to fix anything very ambitious will only make you downhearted if you don't live up to your resolution. So, simple and nourishing is the best rule. I go along with the concept of the nutritious breakfast that's supposed to give you at least a quarter of your day's nourishment. You can fix and eat any number of ideal breakfasts in ten minutes. They should have enough variety not to bore you to death. If orange juice, toast, and coffee every single morning don't bore you, and your heart is set on them have them—and take a vitamin pill besides. But a more luxurious breakfast is more likely to give you the feeling that your day's work is more worth doing. On a cold winter morning, why not, besides the orange juice, toast, and coffee, also have a dish of steaming-hot instant Cream-of-Wheat, into which you toss a few raisins along with a dollop of butter and some hot milk? Instead of toast some morning, why not a toasted English muffin with apricot or raspberry conserves? And a scrambled egg, while you're at it. A nice idea is to keep bakery rolls in the freezer. While you're dressing and making up, have one thawing and warming in a low oven with the oven door open; orange juice, a hot, crisp, buttered roll with a bit of Gouda cheese, and coffee in that china cup make a very good breakfast.

You have probably noticed that all these little variations I am suggesting contain protein. Presumably you know all the foods that do, and how they nourish you, so add them whenever you can: eggs, cheese, bacon, cereal, and so on.

As for Saturday and Sunday breakfasts, you have more time, and you've probably worked hard all week, so you owe yourself something more luxurious than weekday breakfasts. Broiled pink grapefruit, bacon and eggs, rolls and hot coffee, for instance. Or start with a whole peeled orange on a plate, and eat it with a knife and fork. Have your weekend breakfasts on a tray in bed, or have them at a table beside a window with a view or without a view. A good pattern, if you can discover a good bakery in your neighborhood, is to do as a friend of mine does: She wakes up early on Sunday morning, has a cup of hot tea in bed, then dresses in slacks and sweater and goes to a French bakery where she buys one brioche and one croissant. Back home, having had an appetite-creating walk and a sniff of morning air, she luxuriously settles down at a small table in her living room and has a delicious breakfast that is so calorie-filled that on second thought I have decided not to describe it at all.

You'll be less reluctant to fix any meal if you have a snug little kitchen to fix it in. And convenient and pretty pots and pans. The rules are simple: You have only to remember that any kitchen pot or pan that is recommended to you by knowing salespeople for "just one person" is always too small. Have a few pots and pans that are really big enough; and they might as well be pretty, with white forget-me-nots on blue enamel, or orange pots with violets on them. Have a frying pan and a cooking pot with glass covers so you won't have to keep lifting the cover a dozen times to see how the food is getting along. Have a pretty apron of the bib kind, and with a pocket, and have everything you use most often (like the can opener and spatula and tongs) hanging from hooks above the counter. Good things to hang on the walls are a child's slate and chalk for writing down things you need, and a rack of favorite cookbooks, a few pictures, perhaps a hanging plant, and anything else you see in stores' culinary departments and fall in love with.

If you have a dearth of counter space, cover a packing case with flowered contact paper and use it as an extra side table. You can turn a live-alone kitchen into a little jewel with practically no effort at all, what with contact paper and paint and copper this and that. A shaded wall lamp above the counter top makes everything much prettier, and you're better able to aim for cutting the onion and not your fingers. And if you put your dinner plates on a rack on a shelf right above the lamp, if that's where your shelf is (that's where mine is), the lamp keeps your dinner plates warm, à la expensive restaurants like Lutèce or La Caravelle. Convenient things to have *on* the counter are a wicker picnic basket or the like, in which you can keep piled up grapefruit, oranges, and even onions and potatoes; a glass full of cutting knives (with the handles up, of course) and a jumbo-sized salt shaker and pepper grinder. Keep a corner for your idiosyncrasies, too . . . in my case a tiny balloon brandy glass holding saccharine tablets, and a Dijon mustard pot holding vitamin capsules (so there is no top to bother unscrewing).

The kind of food you cook for yourself in this kitchen should be, as I suggested some minutes ago, of the best quality. If you are going to have one lamb chop, buy the most fabulous chop. And buy it from the best butcher. The next night you can make up for it by having a tunafish-and-rice casserole. Or maybe the next three nights, the price of lamb chops being what they are. Keep in mind, by the way, that you do not owe allegiance to any butcher. You have not taken a loyalty oath to patronize him, and at the current prices of meat he is lucky you are buying meat from him at all (and for that matter, so are you). So if there is a good supermarket sale of any cut of meat good for stewing or braising or any other way you like it, seize the opportunity and shop there. That generally means buying a larger quantity, but you needn't worry about leftovers—not if you make, say, enough beef stew for four, and ladle the other three portions into plastic containers, and freeze it, so you have three meals for later on. Next to the woman's liberation movement, the invention of the freezer has done more than anything else to make the live-alone life breezier and more beguiling. All the one-person-sized cans of food have, too—small cans of tongue, chicken, various kinds of fish, and all the frozen foods and vegetables that can be dressed up and made delicious. I am not including frozen "TV dinners," which I feel ought to be stamped out, like the tsetse fly, and I hope you are never tired enough after a day's work to buy one. You would do better to splurge by telephoning the nearest good delicatessen-restaurant and having them send in a hot meal. Having a dinner sent in occasionally adds variety anyway, and it is a luxury that, I hope, you can occasionally afford.

Then there are Saturday noontimes and Sunday four o'clocks, when you're in the mood for an unidentifiable simple something—but what? You are more likely to know if you keep a list of your favorites; otherwise it is surprising what good things you can forget. You may love a baked apple with a golden rim of maple sugar on top and a glass of cold milk—but you might forget it for a whole year, unless it's on your list. Put it down. And put down those other things that escape you, whatever they may be—cinnamon toast and tea; graham crackers with hot milk; liverwurst on a seeded roll; hot tomato soup with a cucumber sandwich. An English girl from Eastbourne, who now lives in New York, tells me her favorite is something called a "Boer War" sandwich, but that it had slipped her mind for years. She swears that her grandfather was in the Boer War, and that that's what he told her the soldiers loved to eat, and it was *his* favorite meal, and it is now *her* favorite, particularly when she is short of money. It is a tasty dish for anyone's list. The recipe is to beat up 1 egg with ½ teaspoonful of mustard and 1 tablespoon of butter or margarine, then add salt to taste and 1 cup or less of grated hard cheese, stale or otherwise. Put this filling between two slices of plain bread and then fry the sandwich in a frying pan with a bit of butter until the filling is cooked and the bread is crisp. A pot of hot English tea goes with it.

You can even have fresh vegetables, provided you learn which ones keep practically forever. A head of cabbage goes under the heading of forever, since it keeps for six weeks to a couple of months, and you always thereby can have a cupful of instant cole slaw or a wedge of hot buttered cabbage sprinkled with grated Cheddar or Parmesan and black pepper. Carrots last for months in the refrigerator, and you can even buy a butternut squash that lasts a month, and that's big enough for eight people . . . but since you are only one, you merely slice off an inch of it, cook it in an inch of water, drain it, mash it with butter, and sprinkle with nutmeg. It is ideal with cole slaw (from that long-lived cabbage) and with roast chicken, for which the recipe is to buy a chicken, put it in the oven to roast at 325 degrees, and go to the movies. When you get back, it will be done. A five-pounder takes three hours or so, and your cookbook tells you how long other weights take. Choose the piece you want for dinner, and wrap the rest in plastic wrap for other days when you'll eat it as chicken sandwiches or a salad with hot rolls on another night, or whatever other way you like. We mention this roast chicken because we know too many live-aloners who feel they have to deprive themselves of whole birds. But buying a sizable chicken is not at all equivalent to investing in a whole cow.

Then there is dieting. Dieting, when you live alone, is much simpler than when you live with other people. Whatever food is brought into your apartment is brought in by you, so you needn't be faced with other people's calorie-riddled favorites every time you open the kitchen cabinet—things like macadamia nuts, peanut butter, marshmallows, and chocolate cookies. And at mealtimes there is nobody eating banana-cream pie three feet away from you. Neither are you preparing rich meals for others, and wishing self-pityingly that you too could eat them. Obviously, then, you should be able to diet so easily that you look like an advertisement for wheat germ or miracle vitamin pills. That's how healthy and slender you should be.

But are you? If you are falling down on the job, sometimes it is a matter of being too hit or miss—like the fabled dieting lady who couldn't ever slim down, the story goes, though "She used to diet on any kind of food she could lay her hands on."

The point here is that since you can select exactly the foods you want to stock your shelves with, you need only the knowledge and fortitude to stock them with the right things. If you are shaky about your calorie and nutrition knowledge, the best little booklet to have on your cookbook rack is the "Nutritive Value of Foods," Home and Garden Bulletin No. 72, which you can get for 30¢ by writing to the U.S. Department of Agriculture, Superintendent of Documents, U.S. Government Printing Office, Washington, D.C., 20402.

Little calorie savings save a lot. Some people think they must eat a whole can of whatever they've just opened, even if it's a quantity for two people because they think it will go bad. Or that it's "so little anyway." A little more is a little too much. Besides, a leftover half-can of food is safe to keep even in the opened can, says the Department of Agriculture, as long as you keep it cool and covered. Even when an acid food like tomatoes dissolves some iron from the can it isn't harmful or dangerous. And of course you can freeze the food anyway. You can eat a half-can of a 3½-ounce can of tuna fish and freeze the other half. Whoever said you have to think in terms of eating a whole anything, anyway? An orange, for instance, which is 50 calories, or a small apple, which is 64 calories? No need to eat a whole apple or orange, though most of us do, on the same principle as people climb the Matterhorn: because it's there. You'll be surprised how many calories you save by eating half. If it's fresh fruit, wrap the other half in a twist of plastic wrap as a before-bedtime snack. You might, once you start "halving," try it lots of ways. At breakfast, for instance, fill an eight-ounce glass with four ice cubes and four ounces of orange juice; it will *look* like eight ounces, but you're saving 55 calories. Pineapple juice? You save 65 calories. Grapefruit juice, 50 calories. And so on.

While I'm on the subject of dieting, at breakfast whenever you have a bowl of wheat flakes or such, try topping it with delicious bits of strawberry-banana gelatine dessert of the low-calorie kind, at 5 to 10 calories, instead of a sliced banana, which is 100 calories. And I assume that of course you're using skimmed milk, and, instead of sugar, a drop of saccharine. There's no need for you to have sugar in your apartment at all, except possibly a minimum amount, concealed on a high shelf from your casual glance, and to be taken down only for guests. Or whole milk, for that matter.

Beyond these few suggestions, I am of the school that believes dieting is most successful and life is happiest when you partake of all the good things in life, gastronomically and otherwise. This may sound as though I'm backtracking; nevertheless, you can eat anything you please if you discipline yourself enough to eat only small portions of it. Living alone makes it easier to eat smaller meals; for one thing, your dinner can be as unhurried and reposeful as you like—and when you eat slowly, your blood sugar has time to rise, thereby satisfying your appetite and leaving you with a nice glow of satiety (you may find you even want to skip dessert). Physiologists say that if you take at least half an hour to eat an average dinner, it will do the trick; that you'll feel satisfied, which is why slow eaters are usually slender, even though they spend more actual *time* at the table than other people. You'll also eat smaller portions if you keep a fashion magazine at hand and take the trouble to glance through it at the skinny models before eating. When I was a fashion editor and attended the big luncheons at which the seasonal fashion collections were shown, I used to wish the models would come down the runway *before* luncheon, instead of after—and I can still hear the regretful sighs of the diners around me who had just eaten a rich luncheon and were now viewing enviably wraithlike models.

It helps to know all kinds of basics, such as that when you diet on high-protein foods like steak, chops, roast beef, fish, and poultry you shed fat faster than when you diet on high-carbohydrate foods like peas. Statistically, proteins and carbohydrates have the same amount of calories: but when you eat protein you increase your metabolic rate, which burns up calories faster, whereas when you eat the same caloric amount of carbohydrates, you're more likely to end up storing some of it as fat. The *highest* carbohydrate foods are corn, white or sweet potatoes, fresh peas, fresh lima beans, and they all contain from 18 percent to 21 percent carbohydrate. You needn't worry about the rest, though—they range from 9 percent down to only 3 percent. Among the 3-percenters are greens, cabbage, cauliflower, summer squash, tomatoes, zucchini, and spinach.

It also helps to know that while a half-pound of beef has about 1,000 calories, a half-pound of a flat fish like sole or flounder has only about 200 calories, and as much protein as meat. Besides, fish is inexpensive compared to meat. With a little practice in the kitchen, you ought to be able to make quickly the sort of dishes for which seafood restaurants charge such frighteningly high prices. They are not charging for the wedge of lemon and the sprig of parsley or even the sliver of fish, but for their know-how. So why not emulate it at home, with a little fish cookbook or even your regular cookbook? Try delicately broiled scallops with a green salad, or sole brushed with a garlic sauce, and try a few new and unfamiliar fish dishes.

If you're the type who's usually ravenously hungry before a meal, you'll eat less if you start the meal with soup; it really *does* fill you up. A low-calorie bouillon has about 8 calories, and even a dieter can have it with a dash of sherry, since the alcohol in the sherry evaporates when you simmer the soup, doing away with the calories in the wine, but leaving a heavenly flavor. A marvelous bedtime snack is a cup of low-calorie bouillon in which you let a saltine soak for five minutes; the saltine swells to four times its bulk. You can make a bedtime cupful seem luxurious as a maharajah's dish, by adding a dollop of whipped-cream-looking yoghurt —it has only 7 calories to a tablespoon—and you are living sleepily and royally for a total of only 30 calories. Or if your bedtime hunger is the sweet-toothed kind, then curl up with a 9-calorie cupful of that gelatine dessert I mentioned earlier, maybe raspberry, orange, or strawberry. It will do more for you than a security blanket.

Whether you diet or don't, we are insistent about nutrition for the simple reason that there is no room in a live-alone life for lying around Camille-like or with constant colds and unnecessary ailments. The live-aloner I can think of who is in the glowingest of glowing health does not, I notice, eat different foods from other people, but she does make a point of eating *synergistically*. She is in her late twenties, the daughter of a well-known nutritionist, so she knows what she is about. She is careful to eat certain foods together, since they yield up more nutrition that way: cereal and milk do; so do bread and milk. Bread and meat are more nutritious when you eat them together. So are eggs and toast. "Synergistic" is from the Greek, meaning "work together" and it means that the total effect is greater than the two things working separately. When you eat foods with a high-protein value, like eggs, fish, milk, meat, and cheese, at the same time as you eat a cereal or grain such as bread, the high-protein food "rounds out" the lower-protein food, and you get more nutritional value. This twenty-eight-year-old is slim as anything yet she eats potatoes and bread, and she can eat less of anything without worrying at all about nutrition. It would be a matter of wisdom for you to do the same.

But if you do get a virus or the latest flu germs going around, and have to go to bed with it, you may as well make the most of it. Have a cut-glass pitcher of fruit juices on your bedside table. At night time, baby yourself with mugs of hot cocoa, and in the afternoon with tea and lemon. Telephone a friend and have her (or him) bring in some of the most gourmet types of frozen little chicken pies, blueberry tarts, and other delectables and tidbits that will fan your wish to live. If the friend insists on preparing your supper, graciously allow it, since it consists of not much more than turning on the oven, anyway. The friend might as well bring along a few good paperback mysteries for you to read while she (or he) is at it. With all this care and sustenance, you should thoroughly enjoy being sick. You'll also enjoy it even more if you look beautifully sick rather than miserably sick, especially if the obliging friend is male—and even if there is no obliging friend at all, and you have to have all those tidbits delivered from the grocery. Start out with fresh sheets and pillowcases; dust the sheets with baby powder, perfume the pillow, and go languidly to bed in your prettiest nightgown. You have all day to recline against pillows, grooming yourself, brushing your hair, pumicing your elbows, pushing back your cuticles, and so on. Put a drop of perfume on a bit of cotton, and slip it down inside a box of facial tissues on your bedside table; the better you get, the more you'll be able to smell it, and it's encouraging (and fragrant) when you do. With books to read and a telephone at hand, you can have quite a wonderful time being sick, and you'll probably get well sooner than pleases you. I would like to mention here that, sick or well, what you wear at home, in or out of bed, has an enormous effect on your morale—which of course you know, but do you *apply* the knowledge? It is so much more ego-lifting when you walk past a mirror, to glimpse someone attractive and groomed, in velvet pants and a Lauren Bacall-type of shirt, than somebody in a terrycloth wrapper that sags in front and bags in back. Women who don't have jobs are particularly mirror-watchers, so they can become quite miserable, due to what they see in the mirror, *en passant*.

Solitary drinking is quite a different matter from the civilized pleasure of solitary dining. Drinking when you're alone in your apartment can turn into that definitely unattractive pattern for which doctors are still trying to figure out the best cure. You may be relieved to know that of the 700,000 women alcoholics in our country, live-aloners are low on the list. But statistics seldom apply to the individual, or so one feels; so instead of feeling recklessly superior, you would be wise to be wary about drinking when you're alone. Few things are so conducive to drinking alone on an afternoon or evening as *ennui,* loneliness, or depression, and I suggest that the first is something you should make it your business to avoid, and the latter two to recognize and accept, without feeling you have to flee from them as though they were a major calamity to be drowned in a glass.

If you are a widow and new to living alone, you may have encountered the problem of having been through some weeks of sympathetic friends and relatives constantly pressing "just one little drink" on you (as happened to me) to cheer you up. I have known a live-alone widow or two, and two or three divorcées who under these kind attentions have drifted into thinking that the more drinks, the cheerier life would be. This is an illusion that is bad for one's looks and liver, and it plays havoc with one's pocketbook. The thing to do, when you're overwhelmed with sympathy, is to take note of the danger right away, and to get busy actively doing something, preferably anything . . . or, as Dr. Johnson said of people in general, "Melancholy should be diverted by every means but drinking."

If you enjoy a drink, as most of us do, there is no reason not to have one, even alone, provided it is related to eating. Perhaps you feel that an ideal solitary dinner isn't complete without the prelude of a drink before dinner, or a glass of wine during it. I know a New England live-aloner in her fifties, who is a smart businesswoman, and after her full day's work she would never dream of having dinner without first relaxing over a highball. I also have a young French friend who looks on a before-dinner highball or cocktail with horror, as something you should call in the exterminator for, but who always has a glass of wine with her meals.

This is all fine unless, . . . though I can think of one erstwhile neighbor of mine who somehow slipped into making double highballs, and finally triples, and as a result sometimes didn't get to eat dinner at all. I am not treating this situation lightly; and, luckily, neither did she. She determinedly made some readjustments of what she terms her "values," and whatever they are, it worked. I know live-alone women who know how to drink, and I know live-aloners who ingenuously think they can get away with drinking cocktails or highballs alone at three o'clock in the afternoon or alone on weekends, instead of socially and sensibly. I can only say I have never met one of these latter live-aloners for whom this confident belief ever worked; they would have been much more likely to beat the roulette wheel at Monte Carlo.

Then there is eating out. Alone. The idea of eating out alone is enough to make most live-aloners flinch. Maybe you have a cozy neighborhood restaurant that doesn't begrudge you a table for one, is reasonably inexpensive, and where you can relax, and in that case you're astonishingly lucky. But more likely the choice is between hamburger counters and chromium-and-plastic coffee shops. These are usually so bad for your morale that you'd be better off to stay home and dine comfortably on a can of peas, and I urge you to do just that. Or perhaps your neighborhood has a ladylike restaurant of the tearoom *genre,* with bland food like popovers and creamed tuna. These are good restaurants for when you're in an invalidlike mood, but how often are you? Yet at least such tearoomy places provide you with a feeling that you won't be mistaken for an eager pick-up if you order a cocktail first. They are not to be undervalued.

But shouldn't a live-aloner occasionally deserve better than that? For instance, an attractive restaurant of the white-napery variety, where there are soft lights, wine and good food, and where you can feel comfortable and unselfconscious, even though you're a Table for One? The table-for-one problem is as much a solitary man's as a woman's, because whichever sex you are, the restaurant views you as economically unfeasible. The only difference is that a woman feels more conspicuous and uncomfortable.

But of course a woman alone can dine out comfortably in one

attractive place or another. One woman friend of mine, an executive secretary to a judge, in a reasonably big New England city, will occasionally decide she needs good food and service, and she is willing to pay for the comfort. She takes a bus to one of the best (but not most expensive) hotels in her city, where the dining room has rosy lights, and the silver is solid. She always asks for the same table, has the same waiter, and she eats lightly but well. She spends about ten dollars, and she can afford this about once a month. The tip she leaves is always one silver dollar and whatever necessary change, depending on the size of the bill. The waiter has started a collection of the silver dollars (which my friend gets at the bank) and gets a kick out of showing them to other waiters, and you can depend on it that she is always recognized, greeted, and gets courteous service.

Hotels are perfect places for live-alone dining, anyway, as you'll find out if you have reasonably good hotels in your city. They generally have more than one dining room, and one of them will probably suit you. Career women and businesswomen have been criss-crossing this country for some years now, and women dining alone at hotels is usual. Traveling on business, I've dined alone in Hilton hotels, Intercontinental hotels, Sheraton hotels, and plenty of others, and without feeling self-conscious. But if you're worried about being self-conscious, take along a book. You might even read it, so choose an interesting one.

But you can also go to a small, sophisticated neighborhood restaurant and be relaxed and welcome. You'll have to make some concessions, though. The restaurant I occasionally go to alone is six blocks from my apartment. It is chic and sophisticated, a glorified ex-bar that is a favorite dining place of successful writers, producers, and other celebrities. That is, it is a famous dining place for such celebrities after 8:30 or 9:00 o'clock, and the true dining hour is closer to 10:00 o'clock. So I go at 6:30. The waiters are free, unharassed, friendly, and I am given one of the best tables— why not, when almost all the others are empty? I have my choice of the best dishes, all freshly prepared, and never get the bad news that they are regretfully all out of anything. I have learned the waiters' names and call them by them. The most famous celebrities who go to this restaurant for dinner at 10:00 o'clock don't get the attention that I do at 6:30.

If you have one or two small, fine restaurants in your neighborhood, there are a half-dozen ways you can make one of them learn to like you. Go on their "slow" night, when they'd be glad to see even a bill collector. And go early. Dressing well helps, as one well-groomed friend of mine found out when her neighborhood restaurant started ushering her to a conspicuous table because, as she later learned, they proudly considered her something of a showpiece. It also pays to patronize the same restaurant, since any restaurateur is happy to have a *steady* flow of money into his cash register, no matter how small (especially on those slow nights). He is even happier if instead of paying for your dinner with a credit card, you either pay in cash or have a charge account, because that means more profit for him, what with no percentage for him to pay to a credit card company. You'll also be practically guaranteed the restaurant's affection if when a man friend asks you out to dinner, you occasionally suggest your little restaurant and bring him there. Or, dining Dutch with a woman friend, bringing her there will seal the establishment's affection for you. But while you are establishing a welcome on their part, it is best to preserve a certain aloofness on yours. Undemocratic as it may sound, we are in favor of not overdoing friendliness with waiters. A certain formality helps your cause a lot better. Be courteous, but be temperate and cool; *never* be chummy, or before you know it you'll be unlikely to demand or complain when you should. Friendly but firm is in order. Have no compunction about sending back food if something's wrong with it. Don't ever be shy about it. We know a very shy young woman who would rather die than send back a dish, and in fact one time she felt she was about to, having eaten her way through an undercooked chicken *en casserole* due to a faulty oven thermometer; she was saved only by the fact that another diner complained in time, and the culinary disaster was discovered. But her rabbitlike timidity earned her a certain careless attitude from the waiters, and she never again got really good service. Good service is something you should be rather a stickler for; what it all comes down to is mutual respect.

The final seal on this good dinner and mutual respect is, of course, the tip. It is important to tip well, without overtipping. Overtipping is supposed to reveal that you have a terrible feeling of insecurity. Maybe it does and maybe it doesn't, but I once knew a waiter who worked at the Oak Room of the Plaza and who confided to me that he looked down on people who overtipped because *he* scorned their insecurity, and he could not therefore resist treating them with a certain negligence. I am simply passing this on for what it is worth. As for undertipping, undertipping is mean, or at best, thoughtless. In this connection, I have to say that many women, live-alone or not, have a double standard about tipping: It is an I-am-a-woman,-so-I-can-tip-less attitude. Women who have this mistaken attitude probably picked it up like a virus, along with other outdated and fossillike double-standard attitudes. With its overtones of *only a woman,* it belongs where all fossils belong: in a museum. The waiter you tip (or anyone else) deserves his proper tip, in other words, somewhere between 15 percent and 20 percent, no matter what the giver's sex.

With these simple rules, you should be able to establish yourself as worthwhile to your chosen restaurant. The best way I know of to afford to eat dinner out occasionally, with flowers on the table, and white napery, is to almost always eat at home.

CHAPTER 13

Physical Security

What with burglaries and related dangers, you may feel a little uneasy about living alone. If so, congratulations. It is wise to recognize dangers . . . unlike one live-aloner I know, who seldom locks her door when she goes to the corner delicatessen, and who boasts that she's not afraid to walk home across town at midnight after a dinner or evening out, because, as she says, "It's safe enough—people exaggerate so about crime." It doesn't take magic powers to foresee trouble in her future.

Crime *is* up. It is up in cities, towns, suburbs. I am not being an alarmist any more than Paul Revere was an alarmist when he alerted the countryside to the British. I am not being an alarmist any more than those people who early on said that Hitler was not just a funny little man with a mustache, and no more than those New Jerseyites and New Yorkers who during the famous Orson Welles radio program called their newspapers to check on whether the Martians really *had* landed. Why *not* check?

It is not scarehead, it is sensible to be cognizant of crime in your city. You should know the facts and take practical precautions. When you do take steps for your security, you get rid of all kinds of formless fears. Fancied fears can be far more hair-raising than a real thief burglarizing your apartment. Yet I have actually encountered an otherwise intelligent live-aloner who refuses to read her local newspapers on the grounds that she doesn't want to know "all that."

Realistic knowledge is in order. Presuming you do carefully read the papers, taking steps to keep yourself reasonably secure is next.

Burglary is one of the biggest problems, and it is more of a problem not because of the loss of valuables the thief might steal, but because of the dangers of encountering him. Nothing works as well at preventing this as giving the thief no opportunity to get in, in the first place. Of course you have a lock on your door, and of course you always keep it locked . . . or do you occasionally forget? Just to check on the negligence of people in general, the New York City Police Department one morning paid an unexpected visit to 150 apartments in Queens and found that one out of every six persons had left an apartment unlocked.

And what *kind* of lock have you? In case you don't know it, a burglar can open a spring lock easily, and you ought to have a really safe lock on your door, such as a double lock or a deadbolt lock. Or some other good burglar-resistant lock. Mine is the famous Medico lock, available anywhere. It is exasperating to thieves, and discourages them from wasting their time trying to get in. Why should they bother, when other apartments are so easy to break into? You need a good chain guard on the door too, good locks on the windows, and enough suspicion in your head to use them always. If you haven't the first two of these, find a good *bonded* locksmith and make the financial investment.

But supposing you do come home one day and when you start to open your door you find it unlocked. Even if you think uncertainly "Maybe I forgot to lock it this morning," don't go in. Turn right around and depart in the direction of the building superintendent, the doorman, or some other person who will enter the apartment with you, just to check. You will be gladder to look a little silly, than to find yourself face to face with a cornered and possibly dangerous thief. If by some mischance you ever are faced with a thief, give up your valuables without a murmur, which is what the police advise. If you are ever sound asleep and awaken to hear a burglar in the room, follow the very wise police advice: Pretend you're still asleep. Let the intruder make off with even the wallpaper, but don't make a sound. After he's gone is time enough to call the police.

It is smart to follow (as we do) the advice of New York's Deputy Inspector Robert A. Hair, who recommends that a woman alone should ask a neighbor or the superintendent or even the building manager to keep an extra check on her apartment for anyone who looks suspicious. Building personnel are beautifully cooperative if you tip them extra-well at Christmas. So do. And deduct it from your income tax. If a neighbor cooperates, you can keep an eye out for her in return, or do her some occasional favor. No matter how courageous you feel, get to know your neighbors and other tenants in your apartment building; it's extra protection. It also helps you recognize who's a stranger and who isn't. A live-alone neighbor of mine got to know other people in her apartment building by offering to take the littlest children around in a group, on Hallowe'en. Another invited the neighbors on her floor in for a 5:00-to-6:00-o'clock eggnog on her first Christmas there. Friendly conversation with familiar faces in the elevator also helps create a little solidarity.

Having long-term relationships with other people around you, besides neighbors, is more precious than diamonds. It's harder, when you live alone in a big city, to create long-term relationships with the mailman, the cleaner, the liquor-store man. But it's not *that* hard. And it pays off in security. Sociologists call city living a "vertical society" as though everyone is isolated, but this is not necessarily true, and it's a lot less vertical when you start making eye-to-eye contact, recognizing people as individuals. I know my mailman in New York better than the one I ever knew in my smaller town, and I know him *by name*. Know the bank clerk by name, know the cleaner by name, the grocer, the supermarket clerks. It alerts them to you as a person. If you go to your neighborhood stocking shop, know the salesclerk by name. Wherever you live, you have the nucleus of a neighborhood, and you can help considerably to form it yourself. Everybody enjoys it a lot more, too, since of course it is better for anybody's ego than is being anonymous. It is accomplished mostly by, when looking at people, really *seeing them*.

You'll also be safer with the security that comes from a longterm relationship with your maid, part-time or otherwise, if you have one. You hardly want a succession of maids, who are practically strangers, drifting in and out of your apartment. How to keep a maid is a minor art. How to keep *which* maid comes first. You can do without a maid who drinks (on the job, that is). What security is there in that, after all? Aside from that, see that you get a dependably honest maid in the first place, or as dependably honest as you can discover, from a dependable source. From then on, treat her well. See that she's covered for Social Security, as she legally should be if she earns fifty dollars or more per every three months working for you, and that there's a good lunch for her in the refrigerator; and that if you're occasionally home when she's there, you don't dog her footsteps. She knows what she's doing when you're *not* there, doesn't she? Pay her well. Give her the standard holidays and vacations according to the National Committee on Household Employment, which differ, depending on fulltime maids and part-time maids, and give her all the other proper treatment recommended by them. Give her the proper supplies she needs to work well with, and leave her good directions, and don't insist she do some particular job she hates, no matter how much that particular job wouldn't bother you. If it doesn't bother you, then you do it.

And don't presume on her time, and don't let her presume on yours. A little formality is in order. There is no reason to be familiar over coffee cups, having a chat, to "prove" you are democratic. Accept the fact that you are. Her life is private. So is yours. If she finds a man's half-used bottle of cologne on your bathroom shelf or a masculine robe in your closet, it is not a basis for a discussion on lover relationships, either hers or yours. She will, hopefully, appreciate all this. So, hopefully, will you.

Perhaps your neighborhood is perfectly safe in the daytime; but streets, suburban or city, undergo a Jekyll-and-Hyde transformation at night. It is nice to be invited out to dinner often, but what about how you're going to get home? "Come for dinner," friends say, though they live four miles away on a dark and leafy street and there is only bus transportation home. The only thing to do is bluntly mention the problem to your hostess: "Who will take me home?" Even if you're invited to an elegant dinner party with *Boeuf Wellington,* if there's no safe way to get home, decline. Declining works wonders, and sometimes even has extra benefits. A hostess begins to take the trouble to see that someone will be available to escort you home. Often the someone is a male guest with a car. If so, it is courteous to repay him by inviting him in for a brandy and coffee. That always makes a pleasant half hour, and can even lead to longer and pleasanter sessions at some future date. Whether a man escorts you home from a party or dinner by taxi, bus, or car, he deserves this courtesy. Most men are as well aware of the getting-home problem for women as you are. Even if a man is escorting you only to your door, make it your *apartment* door, and not your apartment-lobby door. And don't be shy about asking him to escort you up in a self-service elevator and wait until you unlock your door. I've never known a man to like a woman less for it. One man who escorted me home from a dinner party had recently had his apartment cleaned out by a burglar, and he took the precaution of not only waiting until I unlocked the door, but insisted on checking my closets . . . which at least led to my cleaning the closets next day.

Night-time crime cuts into a live-aloner's social life considerably, but there is nothing to do but face the fact that there is four times as much danger at night, city and suburban, as daytimes. Statistics say so, and it's smart to listen. If by some chance you have to be out alone after dark, on foot, use your head about avoiding dark side streets, and map yourself a well-lighted street route home (even if it takes longer), and if somebody wants your pocketbook, hand it over. If you can't afford a taxi and one is available, take it anyway. It is all too bad, but there it is. It is also simple good sense and security to use your first initial instead of your first name on your mailbox—who's to tell if G. stands for masculine George or feminine Gwen?—and if yours isn't listed that way, you should change it immediately.

The same is true in listing your name in the telephone book, because the telephone book is the obscene phone caller's social directory. Probably by this time every woman knows how to handle the obscene telephone call. But to recapitulate: If an obscene call is repeated, tell the caller you are informing the telephone company and the police, and then do so. If you're embarrassed, and think it would be terrible to repeat those awful, obscene words to the police or anyone else, say them out loud a few times until you get used to them; if they sound just as embarrassing after five minutes, report them anyway. The police can often get clues when the type of obscene call dovetails with other calls they hear about. It is *always* better to answer the telephone than not, again on the principle of fancied fears: One live-aloner in New York who is brave in the daytime but tremulous at night, began getting 1:00 A.M. telephone calls every other night for a week, and didn't answer the telephone, on the principle that the call had to be obscene. Who else would call at 1:00 A.M.? "Why should I have to subject myself to *that?*" she asked me indignantly. Finally, though, the ringing phone providing too many sleepless nights, she answered it. The caller turned out to be a feather-brained friend calling from California with news about a possible coast job for her New York friend. She had simply got the time change confused. New York time, she thought, apologizing belatedly, was three hours earlier than California time, not three hours later. Which goes to show.

Above all, *do* be alarmed when you think there's something to be alarmed about. Do cry wolf. People in general are afraid of showing alarm. Most of us are inclined to take an "it's nothing" attitude, rather than risk the embarrassment of looking silly if it's a false alarm. "I *thought* I smelled gas," a patient was reported to have said from a hospital bed after her cooperative apartment blew up, "but I didn't want to say so." If you think you smell gas, you probably do. If you think you smell smoke, that too is likely. A stranger lingering in your lobby? Who is it? Don't worry about being thought woman-alone foolish, when it turns out to be your new neighbor's husband. Better to be an alarmist. Better to raise an alarm, groundless as it may turn out to be, and idiotic as you may look. Do this whether the threat is directly to you or not. Raise an alarm if you think someone outside in the street or next door is in trouble. "I thought someone else would call the police," isn't good enough, tragically, either in fact or in your conscience. Of *course* you hate to do it; but do it. You will also be doing it for yourself, since one excellent way to be safer in your neighborhood and city is to scotch any kind of crime at its inception.

Probably you will never in your life have to call your local police, but even so, tape your police emergency number (in New York and in some other cities it is 911) to the bottom of your telephone. If you're the type that becomes all thumbs in an emergency, you can always just dial "O" for operator and tell her whether you want the police or fire department. Take any other precautions that suit your suburban or city life; if a dog fits your life, maybe you want to consider having one. In fact, you might even want to make a fuss to get better security in your apartment building or neighborhood, even though everybody else around you is slumped in apathy.

As for your own personality and consequent vulnerability, look to it. Distrust is better than ingenuous innocence. Probably from the time you could talk, you have been warned about overly friendly strangers. But are you still listening? Overly casual friendships are the height of unwisdom when you live alone. A rather impulsive young woman mentioned to me recently that she'd met a man at Jones Beach, and had waxed so enthusiastic over him that she'd invited him home for a drink. "But he looked so different when he changed from swimming things and we met at the parking lot!" she said. "He was wearing sharpie clothes and I thought right away: *He's connected with something shady.*" She pretended she'd lost her apartment key, and the date was off. The following week, in reading the newspaper, she discovered that her beach friend was more than shady. He made a practice of meeting young women at the beach, and assault and robbery were the mainstay of his repertoire. Unfortunately, you can't generally recognize danger by the cut of a man's jacket.

I have meant to frighten you into paying attention to your live-alone safety. But I have not exaggerated. And my aim has been to replace your possible unawareness with knowledge, security, and consequently with more self-assurance. You can be altogether more optimistic when you know you've cut way down on the chances of anything ever happening.

Living alone may make you a little edgy about other emergencies. Waking in the night with a stomach ache when you're alone is more alarming than waking up with a stomach ache when there's someone else there to assure you that it is scientifically impossible for you to need your appendix taken out *twice*. There is no one to give you moral support, no one to give you a pill. But qualms of the *Is it really a stomach ache—or a heart attack?* variety are less scary if you keep yourself checked up on. So do so. You know the procedure: a yearly physical check-up, the dentist, the oculist, and all those other costly but necessary measures. And hospitalization, just in case. And a doctor's telephone number at hand.

And even if you hate exercise, unless you do some, you won't be in good enough shape to live alone confidently. If sports don't fit into your life, any kind of exercise will do: dance by yourself in front of the mirror, or clean the bathtub, or vacuum the living-room rug (most live-alone apartments could use a little housecleaning anyway, and the activity gets the circulation going). If the idea repels you, there's always an expensive gym class with chic leotards and foreign accents and socialites, or inexpensive ones at the YWCA. In New York, for instance, the Y offers marvelous value, everything from "Streamlined Gym," classes of exercises done to music (fifteen dollars for eight sessions), to yoga (thirty-two dollars for eight visits). If your idea of exercise is on the less vigorous side, you can have something called "Relaxercize" sessions (eight for eighteen dollars). There's even the exotic Chinese dance called Tai-Chi Ch'uan, slow-moving and beautiful and ancient, but while *it* is ancient, it keeps your body resiliently youthful.

We are not waving a flag for the body beautiful. But we side with the forgotten physical culturist who in the early 1900s suggested that the way for us all to keep in good physical shape is to have one "Naked" national holiday a year, a day in which "Every citizen must go naked into the streets." *That,* he felt, would keep people on their toes. If you can persuade yourself to measure up to how you'd like to look if such a "Naked" national holiday existed (Why not mark an imaginary one on your calendar?), you'll be in good enough physical shape to live alone without qualms.

CHAPTER 14

The
Need
for
Love

Well, here you are: warmhearted, independent, and with an attractive apartment. You have interests, you have activities, you're enjoying life. But . . . what about love?

Caring about other people (and being cared about) is in the same heartwarming class as firelight, hot soup, and a warm coat in winter, and of course you deserve your share. Luckily, all kinds of love, from affection to romantic love, can be in the cards when you live alone.

But if you're going to have love, you have to be receptive to it, graciously bowing it in. It helps enormously if you start by assuming that you have a very good chance of getting some, which of course you have. Live-aloners who have a comfortable amount of love are invariably the ones who go on the assumption that love in their life is as expected as rain in April. (I am thinking particularly of a former secretary of mine who was a good fifteen years older than I, and plain-faced, yet who in the years I knew her, wore this assumption of love like a magic amulet, and it practically *did* work magic.)

The fact is that there is *always* the possibility of love, and age or plainness or anything else doesn't matter. But as any poker player knows, you have to declare yourself in the game, if you're going to have any chance of winning. What I'm suggesting is that if you're open to the possibility of love, you have the best chance of finding it.

Perhaps you already have a man in your life, or maybe with other interests like classes and a career and travel, you're too busy to take the time . . . or you're so much in demand among friends that you feel sufficiently loved. But if not, there are any number of effective steps you can take to get into the game.

If there's simply no man in sight for you at the moment, the best thing is to seize the opportunity to profit by your uncommitted chunk of time. You might start by just checking over what love you already do have in your life. When you do check you'll likely gain considerable confidence and even feel exhilarated, because it is astonishing how much love you can discover you're getting from your family and friends. But maybe you hardly noticed it? I can think of one friend of mine who was feeling wistful about the temporary lack of love in her life; but one afternoon when she made a doodling list with pencil and paper, she was surprised to find that she already had quite a nice amount banked here and there. Her checking bolstered her confidence enough so that when she met a "possible" man a few weeks later, she was able to view the possibility of an impending love affair with a clearer eye.

You might also squeeze in a few hours to give other kinds of love than the romantic variety to people who need it. This isn't as altruistic as it sounds, since caring about other people is a remarkable key to becoming lovable yourself. One warmhearted friend of mine, recently divorced, and with no man yet in sight, has taken on the job of being a New York School Volunteer, and she spends six hours a week tutoring a child. *Free time and love* are the qualifications for the job—you don't even need a high school diploma (or you can be a Ph.D.). "Mine's an eight-year-old named Alicia," my divorcée friend tells me of the child she tutors, "and she's had such a discouraging background that she wouldn't even talk at first, except to answer questions. She was like an automaton. Then one day last month, I was late, and when I came in she was pale. 'Where *were* you?' she asked me. And lately she hugs me. She's become so different!" My friend has since rounded up a couple of her friends and acquaintances to join the program, so the New York organization now needs only about 2,999 more volunteers. Other cities also need hundreds, and even thousands, so there's plenty of this kind of love to give and get. You can't possibly get out of practice.

It is also more profitable all around to use the time to become more attractive, more . . . well, *lovable*. Taking care of your looks and clothes do count for something. It helps in making you confidently expect life to treat you well. And looking good raises your self-esteem so much that it's bound to make you more attractive to other people. One journalist friend of mine is a raw-boned young woman who has become very chic, has cultivated her excellent mind, and attracts an inordinate number of people. They single her out and want to find out what she's like. Perhaps half the people she meets don't even like her (or she them), but at least they try to become acquainted. When you take this much trouble with yourself, it shows you care about people and are interested. It's like dangling a fishline with juicy bait instead of with none at all. And it can be the start of something.

Everything you do *for yourself* generally makes you more lovable. So whenever you're waiting for a possible man to turn up, the best thing is to enjoy positively a life full of activities, friends, humor, and creativity. It isn't even stretching the truth to say that just about anything you do in the way of developing interests and a career, *anything* that builds your self-respect, seems to make you as attractive to men as though they'd inadvertently wandered into a magnetic field. It's not only because you become a more interesting person. It is because <u>when a man is aware that you have interests that you can depend on for sustenance and satisfaction instead of depending on *him,* he can more easily relax.</u> All these interests also help keep you from occasional nobody-loves-me blues that are almost always the result of boredom and that can send you pursuing love down labyrinthian paths that would confuse a mathematical wizard.

It also helps to accumulate gradually a goodly number of platonic men friends. Men make very good friends. And it is very pleasant to have the opposite sex nearby. That's true even if you have a special man in your life. The four or five men in my own life, who are good, platonic friends, are vital to what I think of as the good life. They are men with whom I can talk on the telephone, invite to my parties, occasionally go to the movies or a concert or to dinner with. I remember that Isak Dinesen, that remarkable Danish woman who wrote such marvelous books and best sellers, among them *Seven Gothic Tales* and *Out of Africa,* talked often about the men-as-friends in her life, all her life, into her late seventies. And when she once said, "I have a talent for friendship, friends are what I have enjoyed most: to stir, to get about, to meet new people and attach them," everyone knew she was speaking of her *men* friends. Yet all those men friends were perfectly aware that she still loved her former lover, Denys Finch-Hatton, who was killed when his small plane crashed in Africa.

You don't have to be a fascinating, best-selling personality to have a reasonable number of platonic men friends. A reasonable number can even be two. A man friend is even someone you've met at your office, work with, whose company you enjoy, and with whom you share coffee breaks. One of my closest male friends is an editor I worked with eight years ago. Having male companionship without intimacy is one of the nice things live-aloners can have that is more difficult for other people to have. Living alone, you have the advantage of selecting friends to please yourself only—you needn't have the smallest inhibition about whether your family or a marital partner approves. So go ahead and have as many men friends in your life as you can accumulate.

And be wise enough to get deeply interested in your particular field . . . which is, in its way, a form of love. It can be enormously satisfying. What the writer Katherine Anne Porter calls "this thing" between her and her writing is, as she once said, "stronger than any bond or engagement with any human being." Most of us prefer more human bonds than that, but when you do work at becoming pretty special in your field, you become a much more self-assured person: You gain such a solid-as-rock supply of self-assurance that you never need to accept every invitation just because it comes from a man. You become confidently more choosy about men when you regard your time as valuable. How you divide up your minutes and hours is important. It is important, *anyway*. As my favorite sage, Arnold Bennett, put it, out of the time you have, "you have to spin health, pleasure, money, content, respect, and the evolution of your immortal soul." What's more, everybody rich or poor, dull or bright, has got exactly the same amount as everybody else. Nobody, as Bennett said, "is cut off at the meter."

It is also remarkably and happily true that the fuller your life is, the more you're able to fit a man into your scheme of things. You yourself have probably noticed that the busiest women you know are the ones who find time for a man in their life. So leading a rich, full life before a man comes along works beautifully too.

Come along, though, is hardly the expression. It is a simple, mathematical law, like gravity, that men don't "come along," and unless you're where the men are, you're not going to meet any. This isn't a terrible problem. If you join a travel club or take a university course, go on a business trip, or work for your community, you can't help meeting men. A widow I know in Massachusetts brushed up on her violin playing (she hadn't played in years), joined a small symphony orchestra, and the man she met is the one who plays the French horn. Another friend of mine who worked in an all-women office switched to a job in an engineering firm with an all-male staff. An art-loving friend in San Francisco joined the Museum of Art and was consequently invited to all the art openings, at one of which she met a university art professor who is now her special friend.

If you want to meet men socially, a good rule is to stick to your own personality, your own instincts, whatever you do. If you're the right age for it, and think you can cope with going to singles bars, then consider it. Singles bars have, after all, become quite a usual way of life in some places, like in my upper East Side neighborhood in New York and in lots of other cities. But if you shrink from the idea, never force yourself to go, or you'll be miserable. The same for singles clubs, which are so numerous in cities (and even towns) lately that you'd think Johnny Appleseed had strewn them around. You meet men—but if you don't really enjoy singles clubs (you'll know after one visit if it's for you or not), don't go again.

As for your social life at parties, what you do when you get to a party makes a big difference, as a widow in her forties who is a cousin of a friend of mine found out. She had arrived from the Midwest about a year ago and got a job as a receptionist with an important theatrical agency. She was right away asked to the large cocktail parties given by the firm. They were parties that would intimidate almost anyone, what with their sprinkling of well-known glamorous names and sophisticates-in-general, and they certainly did intimidate the new receptionist who, anyway, had a tendency to shyness. The result was that she always winged directly and thankfully toward the few people she already had met at the office: two or three homosexual scenic designers, a fatherly and august old-time playwright, and one of the office super-seretaries. But after three or four parties, she realized that she had met, as she put it, "Zero number of people. I clung to the 'safe' ones, as though I were at a hurricane, not a party."

After mulling over this realization, she gave herself the courageous program of *not speaking to anyone she knew,* beyond a polite word or two. Instead, she introduced herself to people she didn't know, whether a celebrity or a shy stranger standing awkwardly alone with a drink. She conducted this minor enterprise on a what-do-I-have-to-lose? basis, and it worked like magic. It in fact led to friendships that were valuable later on when in her job she moved up to working on theatrical bookings; and it led eventually to one important friendship.

If you're the type who's anxious or nervous about going alone to parties or dinners, it helps to recognize that everyone (not only you) suffers social qualms to some degree. Even the late Dorothy Parker, of the razor tongue and cynical poetry, used to slip shyly into a room, as though apologizing for being there. Or perhaps you're afraid of being a wallflower? Not long ago, Doris Lilly, beautiful friend of those fabulous Greeks, Onassis and Niarchos, told me that she trembles at the thought of going to a cocktail party alone. "My God! What if I went to a party and didn't see a face I knew? What if the heads all turned, looked at me, and then turned away? What if *nobody spoke to me?*" And at the thought, Miss Lilly paled lily-white.

Or maybe you worry about being tiresome or a bore at a party? If so, tell yourself that your fear is perfectly natural, and that every sensitive person worries at one time or another about being a bore. Katherine Balfour, the actress, told me not long ago that during the shooting of the movie of Erich Segal's *Love Story,* in which she played Ali McGraw's millionairess mother-in-law, she received a telephone call telling her Ray Milland would pick her up in a limousine and drive her out to Long Island for the shooting. By the time the limousine arrived, Miss Balfour was in a state of collapse. *"Intellectually,"* she explained to me, "I understood why I was so nervous; I felt I had to be fascinating for somebody like Ray Milland, and I was so afraid I'd be boring. I know *in my head* that only a boring man gets bored . . . and if a man is dull, Mme. de Staël herself would bore him. But I always feel the burden is on *me.*" So you can see that we all have social insecurities, and that's true whether you're rich or poor, plain or beautiful, old or young. But you win, practically hands down, when you recognize that you won't turn into a pumpkin if not everybody at a party adores you.

But if you want something more solid to hang onto in unfamiliar party situations, even taking simple steps can often help scotch your social qualms. One friend of mine, a young physics teacher, came to New York some months ago from a very small Rhode Island town. She came on the train, diligently reading a small etiquette book all the way. From the day she was invited to her first party, she studied up on whatever her next social engagement was. Whether she was going to another teacher's wedding or a fancy dinner, she read that book. Now that she is confident enough to relax, she says that, silly as it sounds, plain mechanical etiquette-book social know-how gave her confidence. Later on, whenever she went somewhere socially and met a man she liked, she was relaxed enough to forget herself and be interested in *him*.

Some people have social qualms about their looks. *Why can't I look like her?* they think wistfully, looking across a room at a woman with a prettier face or figure. But you can become amazingly more confident if you occasionally remind yourself that chemistry between men and women is marvelously mysterious, has little to do with physical measurements, and that your individuality, *you* are what counts.

It is eternally fascinating to me that a man who thinks he will fall in love with, say, a tall, thin woman, will meet a plump and friendly one at a party, and in casual conversation find himself warmed and happy and growingly interested in her, while a dozen tall and thin women are right there in the room with him, interesting him not at all. It reminds me of the famous O'Henry story about the young man who really believed he loved one young woman who fitted his ideal of what a woman should be—only to fall irresistibly in love with another young woman who upset all his theories about life, and who was exactly the opposite of what he thought he wanted.

As George Eliot, the famous woman writer of the 1800s, put it, "It is a common enough case—that of a man being suddenly captivated by a woman nearly the opposite of his ideal." And how well she knew! George Eliot herself, as a young woman, used to feel so embarrassed at being so physically unattractive that she had even been known to run crying from the room. Yet when she developed her mind and interests, she so attracted the critic George Henry Lewes, that when he got to know her, he scandalized England and Europe by leaving his wife for her and beginning their love affair that lasted twenty-four years, until his death. Two years after that, when she was fifty-nine, she married the rich and brilliant thirty-nine-year-old John Walter Cross, who had fallen in love with her and she with him.

And of course, women too just as often fall in love with a man who's far from their hazy ideal. A woman friend once told me that the only man she ever fell in love with in her life so little resembled her ideal of a craggy-faced and romantically cynical man, that when she was happiest she used to look at him and laugh with pleasure, and he never knew what she was laughing about. *He* was short and round-faced, kind and clever.

Being an older woman these days needn't intimidate you either —as a quick glance at women-in-the-news should tell you. Here is undeniably glamorous Margot Fonteyn, *prima ballerina* at fifty-three; here is Gina Lollobrigida who, when she turned forty, was so delighted with her mature good looks that she said, "If this is what age does to me, let's have more of it." And how to explain the compelling attraction of older women like famous critic and TV commentator Marya Mannes in her sixties? I would lay it to her conviction that age is not important. "There are days when I feel thirty-five," Miss Mannes said not long ago, "and there are days when I feel forty-five and days when I feel even older. But *inside is the same person that's always lived* . . . I am still passionately involved in the process of living and learning." *Passionately involved.* That, too, is something good to remember. It even helps to be keenly aware of the joys of being older, mature . . . as keenly aware, for instance, as Lauren Bacall, who at forty-six, during the Broadway run of *Applause* said, "I feel the cycle of life changing. It's like a second chance, as if my life is beginning again. . . . My eyes are open, my ears are open. All my senses are at work."

You might even feel justifiably smug about possessing the assets of an older woman, among them warmth, good sense, compassion, and poise—not to mention a certain worldliness and sophistication; these are the kind of assets that made the young man Goudeket fall in love with Colette when she was fifty-two. Younger men (Goudeket was in his thirties) are attracted to older women more than most people think. A music-teacher friend of mine who lives in a southern state is in her fifties, and for the past three years has been having a very happy love affair with a man who is more than a handful of years younger than she. She doesn't know for sure how old he is. "I never asked," she tells me. Nor has he asked her what her age is. Neither cares.

If you've been shy about letting friends know you're interested in meeting men, even just mentioning it casually will often spark a dinner invitation from a friend or couple who are inspired to think of a man you might like. It is easy to be too shy or a laggard about this. I can remember that during my first year as a widow, a married woman friend finally telephoned and hesitantly asked if I'd "mind" coming to dinner. My partner, she said, would be an unmarried man. Since I had shown no earlier interest, she had been embarrassed about asking me. But why wait for your friends to bring up the possibility that you might be interested in meeting men, and which they may *never* bring up, when you can (and should) bring it up yourself? Sometimes widows feel, as one widow told me, that it would be "disloyal" to her husband's memory to love someone else later. But we infinitely prefer Miss Bacall's comment, "God knows, Bogie would have been the first to say that I'm entitled to a life of my own."

The very best attitude when you live alone is to acknowledge frankly your interest in men. That's a lot easier to do these days, now that women are beginning to feel so much more worthwhile. Feeling worthwhile makes it a lot easier to like men genuinely, person to person, instead of on yesterday's old-fashioned catch-a-man-to-marry basis. Besides, nobody cares any longer who's married and who isn't. You can do pretty much as you please, and you can usually afford it financially besides. "I go to parties and expect to meet men I like," a San Francisco woman friend of mine tells me. "But I'm not on a campaign! I go because I enjoy parties and love seeing people, and of course that includes men." Her attitude is warm and spontaneous, and in return everybody enjoys seeing her too, and that includes the men she meets, whether they become friends or lovers.

But if you're going to feel this worthwhile and confident with men, you may first have to get rid of some datedly romantic notions about love. You may have been, as most of us were, brought up on the myth that love is all, your *raison d'être*. You may have absorbed the notion, as so many otherwise intelligent women have done (including our mothers and grandmothers and so on, back into misty history) that the thing to do is to "be good, sweet maid, and let who will be clever," and pretty soon *the* man, *the* somebody-to-love-you will appear on a snow-white charger. You don't actually have to *do* anything, except have a nice little token office job, or learn a little something in college while waiting. You don't need to be much more than a flower, waiting to be picked; nothing is more important than being picked.

This is a traditional little fantasy that is terribly prevalent and can hamper you as much as an iron chain around your ankle. Once you recognize it as an oddity of an earlier era that simply harnesses you, you can relegate it to its proper place, which is a league or two beneath the sea. And once rid of this passive-little-flower myth, you have a top-quality chance to become somebody in your own right: You can become self-assured and self-reliant, and actively, deeply, richly involved in important interests. We have seen this work beautifully in the case of a rather inferior-feeling young woman who had been brought up in a small South Carolina city in the tradition that the road-to-love was femininity, and that femininity meant being dependent, helpless, and self-effacing—in short, being a passive little flower. But at twenty-two she was lucky enough to go to live with an aunt in Philadelphia, while attending music school—an aunt who could have doubled as Auntie Mame, with a touch of perhaps Mme. Curie thrown in. Within a few months the niece's self-esteem had risen like something on a fever chart. Most of it was sparked by astonishment over the way people swarmed around her aunt, who was thoroughly self-reliant, self-assured, and about as passive as an active volcano. Yet she was certainly feminine to her eartips. Having noted all this, the niece concluded, as she later said (she is now thirty-five and a successful concert pianist), that she, too, ought to get more out of life and she began working hard at her music and getting tremendous personal satisfaction out of it. And while, as she says, she recognized that love was important, she discovered that "so are other things." The combination of both that she has since found appears ideal.

It is pretty delightful anyway when you find yourself interested in things for your own personal satisfaction, and not as "accomplishments" to win a man with. You're able to get more happily involved in work, hobbies, interests, your apartment, good friends, even one or two bigger-than-yourself world problems.

Naturally, with all those personal satisfactions in your life, when it comes to sex and love it won't be any wonder that you'll be better able to choose what you want and to reject what and whom you please. When your life is that full, you're never desperate. You can say Yes to one man for whom you feel genuine affection, attraction and (hopefully) love. And you can easily, politely decline a relationship with another man who previously, in your compliant-little-flower era you might have felt you should accept.

So, where love and sex are concerned, this freedom-of-choice is, as they say in Arabian Nights' stories, "a jewel beyond price." And you should regard it as possibly your most stunningly valuable possession. A woman who feels there is no love relationship she *has* to have is likely to have a good few that are well worth having. A young woman friend of mine who is a real-estate broker in California does this enviably well, always having happy and tender love affairs. Hers are not undying love affairs, but neither are they a casual ships-that-pass-in-the-night variety. She is a serious and friendly young woman, who is clever and self-reliant and open-hearted, and to whom love is, as she says, "personal." I could never in the world imagine her letting herself be picked like a flower. Nor can I imagine her needing the kind of dreary sexual relationship that has no meaning—one that isn't "personal." She is, you might say, truly selective, a discriminating woman.

A discriminating woman has the pleasure of choosing what she wants and letting the rest go. Even if there has been a desertlike absence of "possible" men in her life for months or even years, she doesn't feel she has to begin a love affair with a man she doesn't really care for, just because he's the only man on the scene. She is also quite aware that a purely sexual relationship with a man doesn't at all fulfill any "need," but that having warm, personal relationships with people do . . . and that the translation of yesteryear's "sex-starved spinster" was really a need of friends, companionship, and worthwhile interests such as absorbed Elizabeth Barrett until at the age of forty she married Mr. Browning, who was then thirty-four. (We have just noticed again what an extraordinary number of actively interested women *do* marry younger men.)

If you have a family that views your live-alone state as mortifying to them because you're not married and who would rather see you married on any account, you can good-humoredly take their pressuring in stride when you're a discriminating woman. "My family doesn't care *who* I marry," a New York assistant dress buyer in her thirties tells me; she feels *very* worthwhile however, and she is having a happy love affair with a man she doesn't want to marry, at least not yet, and she says there was a time when her family's pressure to marry made her feel like a fly under a flatiron. "My mother's great ambition *still* is to see a ring on my finger. But now it doesn't bother me; now I know it's *my* life." You're even able to withstand other family pressures, sometimes surprising ones. Last Christmas a live-alone friend of mine received from a loving aunt in Denver a Christmas present of a book on sexual freedom, presumably a delicate hint not to let life pass her by, just in case, married or unmarried.

But when you have the aplomb of a discriminating woman, you can firmly make your own personal decisions about love, despite loving aunts with Christmas presents, the influence of popular songs of the I-Need-You variety, TV shows, your family's opinions, or the actions of the latest romantic heroine in a Broadway play. You can cope equally well with all the sexual viewpoints in literature, such as those that advocate a busy sex life with some nebulous Mr. X., or those that view sex rather like physical therapy. "Was it Nero who declared sex his favorite form of physical exercise?" one reviewer tried to recall wearily after reading his dozenth sexology book. More, you can take in stride the half-dozen different feminist viewpoints on love and sex, and also the antiliberation ones that advise women to act with the independence of a marshmallow or like cuddly little bunny rabbits.

All this running-your-own-show sets you up no end, and gives you a glowingly healthy ego, and a healthy ego is as essential if you're going to be able to love other people at all. You also have the pleasure of not worrying anxiously about a whole galaxy of love and sex problems that bother lots of women. You don't worry, for instance, that the man you met last night on a blind date might not like you if you're not immediately sexually available. You don't worry about living up to some flattering and romantic conception some newly met man has of you; you simply don't bother to play out the role.

Altogether, you become very much your own woman. A Massachusetts friend of mine, forty-five, recently divorced, and having just started an already thriving little four-page shopping newspaper in her town, tells me that as a girl she felt so unsure of herself that she probably married her husband because she didn't want to hurt his feelings by saying No. "I was always, all my life, oh-so-willing to please men—I needed their attention and praise." But now, she tells me, "Now I'm beginning to care more what *I* think of *them*."

With an attitude like that, whenever you meet a man you're more likely to have the courage to *take your time* about love and sex and thereby reap all the benefits and have all the enjoyments of the two of you getting to know each other beforehand. The pleasures are so myriad, involving everything from movie-going, to parties, political arguments, exchanging beliefs, and socializing with your friends and his, that it would be a shame to miss them. It also involves feeling generally pleased with yourself, and it is all, as Ben Hecht once said, even good for your vocabulary, as you carry on imaginary romantic conversations with your lover-to-be when he's not there, as the attraction develops. And an attraction worth something is more likely to develop when you take the trouble to know the real person. I can't think of anything more genuinely flattering to a man than showing that you want to know *him* as a person and not just because he's a member of the male sex. It sorts him out as a man who's distinctive and separate from all other men, as singular in his own right as Captain Ahab or François Villon, which every man really is. He's even likely to return the compliment and see you as a unique woman, too, which is a delightful state of affairs all around. This kind of enjoying a person for himself is a far cry indeed from the earlier-mentioned ships-that-pass-in-the-night relationship. And in taking the long, scenic route, you give mutual attraction the best chance to grow into love, like from caterpillar to butterfly. Not that there's a guarantee. But even if the attraction doesn't turn into love and you should decide on a love affair anyway, it can't help but involve genuine feelings and caring, gaiety, friendship, and lovingness. It will be worth having.

As for knowing a man "well enough" beforehand, exactly how well *is* well enough? You'll never find out from a book or even your best friend. You have to figure it out for yourself. You have probably made a mistake or two on that score already, and probably will make one or two more. How you decide depends partly on the man, who is, after all, not an outline image labeled "Man," or a piano on which you're playing a tune (though we have met women who think otherwise), but that real person with his own reticences and foibles and special personality.

It even depends partly on your age and experience with love. A twenty-three-year-old not long ago told me that when she was twenty and studying at a Boston college her idea of "personal" had been to know a man "just barely well enough" to be sure of some weeks of relatively pleasant sex. But after a while, those relationships, which had been new and novel because sex itself was new and novel to her, became boring. Finally, their impersonality began to depress her. Now at twenty-three, she is demanding somebody, "*real,* as part of my life, even if it's only temporary." She is willing to take time for a real person; for a relationship that's richer, rarer. Being young and curious when you *are* that young and curious is one thing. But presuming you are at last an adult woman, you really owe yourself a rich and adult love affair.

I haven't been implying it is easy to control impatience, what with natural sexual desires and longings, and perhaps with only an occasional man on the horizon, but it certainly is 110 percent easier when you're busy with those outside interests we've been talking about. And also when you think of the benefits of a little control.

The great and unparalleled benefit I haven't yet mentioned is that you're likely to become more spontaneous in love. And being spontaneous in love is the best thing about it. This phenomenon astonished one woman friend of mine, to whom it happened. It happened to her a little late, because up to the time she was in her late thirties, she was old-style defensive and self-effacing in the clinging-vine way. She had few interests and when she met men she had only the most desultory week-long "affairs" with them. The affairs were all so disappointing that she couldn't understand "what people saw in sex." Turning away from it with some bitterness and a great deal of scorn, she made an effort to become more interested in her work, which was speech therapy for children. In a couple of years she became pretty exceptional in the field, and was asked to give a series of lectures, at one of which she met a male professor in the same field. By that time she was getting fun and excitement out of her career and was involved in drumming up a national movement concerning her work. For the first time in her life, she had enough plain guts to "see" how well she liked a man first. What she did see, as the pair started meeting over coffee cups and in restaurants and lending books back and forth, was that she could talk honestly with a man and express herself (moreover, she finally had something to say). Her defensiveness dropped away, and with it went the last withered remnants of her clinging-vine tendrils, presumably never to be seen again. With *them* also went her self-consciousness about sex. You might say that for the first time she felt secure enough to be spontaneous in love-making. This particular woman spoke to me of it only once, and very simply, but with such a sense of wonder that it was unforgettable.

Once you declare yourself in this game that I've been talking about, you discover that it is not at all like a poker game, or like checkers or chess, in which you win or lose. In *this* game, you can always win something. And often quite a lot.

CHAPTER 15

Affairs

There is no rule that says you have to have an affair. But if you do have one, it ought to be one of the happiest and most successful in town, even in a large town.

There are certain things that make some live-alone affairs thrive remarkably while others rapidly go where the snows of yesteryear went. I am speaking of affairs for live-aloners, whatever their age, and whether it is a first affair or a much later one.

I ought first to define what I mean by "affair," a man friend of mine having recently mentioned to me that he's never really been sure what an affair is, or when you're in one or out of one. The kind of affair I am talking about is just about any love-and-sex relationship of a reasonable length of time, with some genuine feeling. Or it can even be a love affair that goes on for thirty years, like the affair between Lloyd George and Frances Stevenson.

You might get into your affair by any of a thousand routes. You might even, as Hollywood screen writers used to call it, "meet cute"—that is, get caught in a revolving door together, or bump heads in a restaurant when *you* drop something and *he* picks it up, à la Cary Grant. But that isn't too likely. Most women meet a man at a friend's dinner or party, there's an indefinable attraction, and you recognize that something particularly nice is likely to develop. Or you meet a man and gradually get to like him tremendously: no fireworks, but lots of growing affection, then stronger emotions, then an affair. But you never can guess how you'll meet a man, or where, or how you'll feel. I once knew a woman who romantically took a month-long trip to Europe hoping to fall gracefully, poetically in love in distant lands . . . only to come home disappointed and the very next day meet a new man in her business world; the attraction between them flared into instant conflagration.

But however you arrive in an affair, it ought to supply all those good things that popular word "soul" covers. An enviable affair goes with the smell of freshly roasted coffee, and it goes with telephone calls at certain times of the day, and with making love, and going to the movies, and it goes perhaps with two-handed bridge. It goes with exchanging ideas, and with getting away to Grenada or Puerto Rico or some snowy ski place or quiet inn for a weekend in winter. It also has disagreements and occasional dramatic exits (his or yours). It goes with sharing your thoughts and feelings. *Sharing* is its best part.

It also includes some risks and exasperations and worthless sides. But it has wonderfully intoxicating aspects that make up for those first three. A good affair always reminds me of that Philip Barry play in which our hero asks a sedately married woman to run away with him; he admits that he can't offer her security, but only precarious finances and sometimes bitter quarrels, and excitement and daring and love. So off she runs with him. The curtain comes down and the women in the audience sigh with envy. The point I am making here is that there's nothing like going into an affair with your eyes open, perfectly cognizant of the risks—but much more attracted by the delights.

A live-alone affair has lots of risks, but plenty of advantages. It is, for one thing, an unadulterated feeling between a man and woman. Since you are not obliged to play lots of roles like parttime housekeeper, mother, wife and so on to this man, you are sheerly you, a *woman*. Neither is he, to you, a breadwinner and so on; he is sheerly *man*. There you are. *En face* as Adam and Eve.

Then there is the reason you are having an affair at all, which is a simple one: you want each other. You come together for love, for sex, for talk, for the enjoyment of being with the other person. You're together, when you *are* together, out of feelings. There isn't a single obligation in sight, no social pressure or legal pressure to lock you together one single minute more than you want to be. In fact, society in general still frowns on affairs, at least in most small towns I know of. That even relieves you of the slightest obligation to make an affair "work" as though it had a social purpose. Your only purpose is love. So nothing can keep you boxed in an affair that no longer pleases you—you're free to end it with a word. Not for you the complexities of divorce.

That particular freedom is one thing that makes an affair so fascinating—and so tightrope-walking. The two are as entwined as a braid. It makes for a certain tension that keeps you up to the mark; as a dramatic Russian beauty I know who is having an affair with a symphony orchestra conductor put it, "Neither of us dares to take the other for granted, we are as alert as in a fencing match." As for the sexual and romantic advantages, in her words, "How can your meetings not be prized, when you must even make appointments to be together?" and she sighs for women whose husbands, she believes, seldom bother to say *I love you*. "An unimaginable situation in an affair!"

If you're a social rebel, an affair provides an element of hazard that can even make it sweeter. One friend of mine mourns the fact that she doesn't have to keep her affair a secret, which, she says, would be lots more pleasurable. She is a little irritated that her family heartily approves, and likes the man into the bargain.

Living alone, you also have a dizzying number of aesthetic advantages. You have, for one thing, privacy whenever you want it. Privacy to use hair curlers, privacy when you look swollen-nosed because of an allergy or cold in the head. Or privacy simply because you know you're in a shockingly nasty mood. Privacy! You can be incommunicado simply by picking up the telephone and *saying* you are incommunicado. This latter, of course, is one of the great pleasures other people don't have, but live-aloners do. It means that you can confine slenderizing exercises and eyebrow-shaping to when you're alone. . . . Or, as one woman who is having an admirable affair said to me, "I don't care to have Eric see all the components that go into making up me." When you live alone, there's no reason an Eric ever should. The main thing I have to say about privacy in an affair is that you should guard it like good vintage champagne and your right to vote.

With all these advantages, you should be able to get an affair off to a marvelous start. But of course the point is to turn the fledgling into a full-grown, satisfying affair. The idea isn't to have an affair. It is to have a wonderful one.

With that in mind, I suggest you consider making an emotional commitment.

The fact is, you can't stand in the doorway, hanging onto the doorknob, and with one foot in and one out expect much of an affair. If a man is worth your having an affair with at all, he is worth your making an emotional commitment. That is, being wholehearted about it.

Perhaps you are wary of being wholehearted because you feel that once you make an emotional commitment, you're too vulnerable? Lots of women do feel this way, afraid they might be left in some pathetic or infuriating situation—which of course can happen, and often does. Or that once they're committed, they can't so easily change their mind. So they remain indecisively in the doorway. But *of course* you can give; and then later you *can* change your mind, depending on what emotional changes occur in the affair. And you can *still* say goodbye with infinitely fewer complications than if you were in a marriage.

And, come the Flood or the Millennium, maintain your independent attitude. It enhances your value no end when you're not so easily available, on tap as a glass of water. Not to mention that it gives an affair lots more style. A young woman friend of mine who's in the dress-designing business goes fairly regularly to Cleveland on business and she used to bemoan having to be away from the man with whom she was having an affair—until she discovered that her absence made him regard every minute with her as that much more precious. Now it pleases her to pack her suitcase and fly off to Cleveland.

People do prize something more highly whenever they have to surmount barriers to reach it; and the challenge is so attractive that, as Freud pointed out, "Where there are not barriers, men have always set up artificial ones." Even as a child I recognized this very well when I used to bury a "treasure" (my mother's old junk jewelry, in a cigar box) in the nearby woods and set up all kinds of obstacles to reaching it, including a trench I spent a whole day digging to make the approach more difficult. And look at Don Quixote —he even *imagined* obstacles in the way of reaching maidens. In a more contemporary vein, being unavailable not only makes you more prized, but your personal affairs get done, and your independence remains strong as the Rock of G. Independently taking care of your personal affairs also keeps you from being a suffering martyr about sacrificing your own obligations to accommodate *his* business schedule.

Absolutely nothing is so unattractive in an affair as a suffering martyr. A brand-new-to-an-affair widow who did this for several weeks discovered that all her noble sacrificing was making her secretly so exasperated and resentful that she was building to breaking off the affair; but instead, as she told me, she took a week's vacation in the Caribbean, where, while tanning on both sides, she decided to turn over a new leaf. In fact she turned it over so well and became so attractively independent that she spoiled the affair by marrying the man. To my knowledge they are still living happily (and very independently) ever after.

There is always a certain charm you have for a man when you make decisions on your own—all kinds of decisions that you can freely make because you're a live-aloner, a resilient person-on-your-own. One woman I know, who is having a happy affair, one afternoon had a baby-grand piano delivered without previously even mentioning it, and announced she was henceforth taking lessons two evenings a week. I know another woman who unexpectedly went off on a month-long geology trip, and a third who took a public relations job that involved her being away in Paris ten days every month. Was she missed? Ah yes; yes indeed, she was missed. So if you are tempted to dependently "turn over" your life to the other person (and I have seen one widow even turn over her checkbook to the man to balance it for her), make your own decisions, no matter what.

In that connection, your very best move is to *not* depend on the man involved for your happiness. This is somewhat difficult if you have been brought up, as so many of us have, to expect a lover-daddy-husband perfect all-in-one love from a man. It is an insidious belief that most little girls get in childhood, right along with whooping cough and measles, via well-meaning but fantasy-imbued mothers, fairy tales, and overly romantic novels. On this diet, you can come to expect too much of a man. You can get to believe that happiness comes wrapped in tissue paper in a beribboned box, to be delivered by him. A staggering number of women *do* believe that if a man loves her, he will understand her, bear with her foibles, be loyal, reliable, loving, always in good humor, and will drop everything to be at her side. An Eagle Scout pales in comparison.

Good sense tells us that the Eagle Scout lover is an impossible fantasy, and unless you get rid of this impossible dream, you can find yourself terribly disillusioned to discover that instead of opening a beribboned box you're involved with a man who's perfectly capable of forgetting you're giving a cocktail party on Tuesday, or who gets annoyed when you say you'll pick up the plane tickets and then don't, or if you flood his car engine. It leads in turn to blaming him for this or that, such as why is he in Detroit this weekend, and so on. And then in turn he's liable to feel owned and exasperated and drained, and even exploited, and it's goodbye to a potentially good affair (and is just as bad in a marriage, too).

It is all a terribly easy trap to fall into, given those early childhood expectations. But you're impervious to the trap when you recognize it. Once you do, you can develop the strength, wisdom, and style to depend on yourself: In a word, you can assume personal responsibility for your happiness, gaining it from your goals and your interests, and all other parts of your life, instead of pinning the responsibility on another person. And when you do, the results are spectacular. Nothing scintillates in the sky, but something does in an affair. It is quite a different story, you discover, to love a man not through "feminine dependency" (there's no such thing anyway—it's all in our heads) but *out of one's own wholeness*. It's a veritable gold thread running through the affair.

Besides, a man relaxes better when you're not concentrating on living through him. He already has plenty of problems. This is especially true if you're an older divorcée or widow. At that age, most of the available men in your life have been married or divorced or separated. They have all been burned, and they hurt. *This* man may seem a tower of strength to the outside world, *that* one is as urbane as Clifton Webb, a third appears as wise as an Eastern sage. Yet *this* one has been bruised and has resentments, *that* one has been left warily hostile, the third is tired of being emotionally drained—and all of them are vulnerable. The man in your affair may not be the ideal man (what man is?). But it is better to think simply *He is my love and my companion*.

Some women, in an affair, are marvels at spontaneously offering their best thoughts and ideas, whether the conversation is on the analysis of decadence in *Cabaret* or how to barbecue a steak. The happy result is two people trying to discover the further reaches of the other person's personality. It is real and stimulating, and, finally, flattering and truly endearing. The more you aim for this kind of exchange, the better. Lamentably, some of us are still entrapped in the belief that men won't like us if we have brains. *Don't be smarter than he is* is a warning that floats like a misty gray cloud over our heads. My best advice is to clear away those mists, if you haven't yet done so.

Lillian Hellman, the playwright, who luckily never had such mists, wrote of her many-years-long affair with Dashiell Hammett, author of *The Thin Man:* "I know as little about the nature of romantic love as I knew when I was eighteen, but I do know about the pleasure of continuing interest, the excitement of wanting to know what somebody else thinks, will do, will not do. . . ." When you share your real thoughts, you become many-faceted to the other person . . . just as Hammett one day told Miss Hellman that he had patterned Nora in *The Thin Man* after her, but that she was also even the silly girl and the villainess.

Even so, every woman has her own private thoughts and reflections. They keep her a private person. They needn't at all be shared. Perhaps if you wanted to confide them to the man you love, they are so deep that you wouldn't even know how. They are really more an essence of your being, something that has evolved as you've gone through the growing-up stages of your life and become a complex person, separate, unique. It is a privacy of mind. It is related to the privacy that gives us time to reflect, to become. I've known some few people who can reflect in a roomful of other people, and some with one other person there.

Like most people, I reflect best when I'm alone . . . and sometimes particularly well on long bus trips, and occasionally for that reason I've taken bus trips through New England: simply to reflect out the window. But the point I am making here is that everyone has some natural reticences, some reserve; and in an affair it is equally wise to relaxedly let them exist as yours alone.

Then there is honesty. Honesty in any love affair is priceless. It makes for a very untroubled brow. And it makes for good feelings between you and the man when you honestly face what you want and think and feel. All in all, honesty can be one of your most attractive qualities. What, for instance, do you honestly want out of the affair? Marriage? Simply an affair? Something that won't "interfere" with your career or style of living? The important thing is not *what* you want, but to *know* honestly what you want.

If you are one of the new breed, maybe you don't want to marry. You may prize your live-alone life above rubies for a variety of reasons, some of which may have something in common with, say, live-alone Gloria Steinem's comment that "I like the infinite possibilities of life. Not knowing what's going to happen has always been my security. I guess that's one of the reasons I haven't married. I once said the word 'marriage' was like a door slamming in my head." Ms. Steinem is in her thirties, and she lives in a three-room apartment on the East Side of New York, just three blocks from me, and both the charm of her apartment and her personality, and the details of her private life are quite well known. Maybe she will marry "someday," as she has said more recently . . . and hers is the attitude of more live-aloners than ever in the last half-dozen years. *Someday.* But not now. *For now, this live-alone life is mine.* Marriage is no longer the big attraction on the marquee.

But whatever your attitude, the most refreshing thing in the world is not only to know your own mind honestly, but to tell the man involved. It is the difference between conducting an affair like a muddy river or a crystal-clear one. One widow I can think of explained it all very well to the man with whom she was having an affair. She had been married twice. Her first marriage was full of problems and ended in divorce; her second marriage was a grand passion. Now, she told the present man frankly, she had learned to live alone and she was enjoying it; she wouldn't part with it for anything. What she wanted was a calm, undemanding affair: someone to care about and love quietly, someone to go to parties with, to be with on holidays, to visit other couples with. . . . And that is just exactly the affair she has been having these past four years with this man who loves her and accepts the pattern.

Another woman who is having an equally frank (but more exciting) affair, is a Philadelphia architectural student. She is twenty-seven and has just turned down the proposal of the well-to-do architect with whom she is having the affair. She has told him honestly, "Of course you matter—but there isn't any man I'd want to see more than four times a week." She lives in a two-and-one-half-room apartment in a dreary part of Philadelphia, while he has an elegant town house. But, as she says, "Mine is my own." Will she ever feel differently? "Oh, *probably* . . . But right now I feel *this* way. I love my life the way it is."

But during your affair, your feelings can change, and it is important to keep the other person au courant. Maybe you start out feeling like this Philadelphia architectural student. Marriage doesn't figure in your dreams at all, at first. But what with one's emotional temperature always changing and the affair evolving into something else, what might have started as an affair of tenderness or basically sexual attraction can turn into a deeper love.

So maybe at some stage in the affair you (you alone) begin to think about the possibility of marriage. If you do, the best thing is to bring up the question quickly. If you do bring it up, and the man doesn't want to marry (or for some reason feels he can't), you at least know the situation. The air is cleared. You can decide to continue the affair anyway, and have a perfectly good and harmonious and loving affair—or you will be furious and end it. Either way, fine. But *not* to ask, *not* to know where you both stand, is too much like feeling your way around a room blindfolded. You need enlightenment. Not to know where you stand can lead to resentments and hostility and can make you needlessly miserable—and can often spoil a perfectly good affair.

Sometimes shyness gets in the way of honesty. One friend of mine was unable to mention marriage out of sheer embarrassment; as she explained: "I felt it would be like asking him to marry me." Or you can be so afraid of being told *I don't love you enough,* that you bury the temptation to find out. Or you have any of a dozen other fears. In that case, it is good to remind yourself that you are two people with good feelings for each other. That makes it easier to be frank. And once you are frank, it contributes mightily to your self-esteem (speaking up when you know you should, always does). And it wins you admiration besides. Then, between you, you can discuss what you both want.

As for having an affair with a married man, you may be among those who say, "Me? Never!" But you'd better be prepared, anyway. Almost every live-alone woman I know who is having an affair with a married man belongs to the "Me? Never!" school. You may avoid married men the way you avoid earthquakes, countries with revolutions, and other dangerous phenomena. But you can't always control what is going to happen. You can get on a New York-to-London plane for a business trip or holiday, and before you even reach Heathrow Airport you will know that even though the man seated next to you and with whom you've been chatting all across the Atlantic is married, you will anyway agree to meet him tomorrow for lunch, because you are already half in love. That was the start of the affair of one of my friends, a widow in her forties. Lunches turned to dinners, she introduced him to her friends in London, and back home they continued to meet in New York. There are plenty of complications, because with a married man there always are. Yet it is what she wants.

You can't even count on your upbringing to help you steer clear of married men. A never-married friend of mine who lives in a small Massachusetts town was brought up on ethical and moral standards as Puritanical as they come—yet ever since she was thirty-seven she has been having an affair with a married man who can't, for some reason, divorce. The affair has been going on for eight years. She has had to be secretive and has had lonely holidays and weekends by the dozens and hundreds. But she says it is worth it and she would do it again, and that when the affair ends that will be all right, too. "We love each other and we decided a long time ago what we wanted."

Knowing what we want. Loving each other. These can make up for the less-than-ideal of such an affair. I have a friend who is a glamorous New Yorker, and sympathetic, loving, kind, and romantic. She has been having an affair with a married man for six years. They, too, are unable to marry, and it is a thorn in their lives. To be together and not married leaves them not quite happy. But to be apart would devastate them. This, I think, is real love. And when it *is* real love, real commitment, it can work.

But it works only under certain circumstances: It is perfectly possible to have a healthily selfish affair with a married man, provided you have a clear-cut understanding. That means you need the answer to key questions, such as *What is so wrong with his marriage that he is here with you?* And *Exactly what relationship does he want with you?* Once you have the answers to your satisfaction, you can perfectly well decide what you want to do about it: an affair or not. If you settle for an affair, I don't need to tell you all the risks and emotional problems involved. However, I can only presume you know what you want. As one friend of mine said of her affair, "We used to be so anxious and guilt-stricken about his wife, even though she doesn't care about him; but finally we decided to go on the premise that what counts is what *he* wants and what *I* want."

Some other women have what used to be called a "masculine" attitude about affairs. One such woman friend of mine, who does not care to marry, steers a very blithe course through affairs with one married man over a period of years, and then with another. But that takes a bent of mind most of us don't have, and you might well become pretty crushed under such circumstances. Still, there may be a time or two in your life when that's exactly what you *do* want, and I have even known such an affair to have a salutary effect. A particularly charming and intelligent Canadian woman was divorced after a very unhappy marriage. Not long afterward, in the process of recovery, she began an affair with a married man. It was not a deep or strong love, and certainly the man intended to stay married. The situation consequently drew the disapproval of several of this woman's friends, one of whom told her she thought it terrible to be "settling for only half a loaf." "But of course!" was the divorced woman's response. "Right now, half a loaf is *exactly* what I want!" And so it was . . . then. But three years later when she was in a more receptive frame of mind, she met a man to whom she is now happily married.

But in the live-alone life, the real drawback to an affair with a married man is that your affair ought to encompass all those enjoyable trips, socializing with other couples, activities, companionship, and fun. A married man has other commitments, and can't so well supply these good things. So naturally it makes better sense to keep an eye on the fact that one good reason for an affair in your live-alone life is the whole delightful sharing and socializing aspect of it. You and your love can't very well drive to the country on Sunday to picnic with friends if he has a wife and family commitments elsewhere. But with an unmarried man you'll seldom have to cast about for whom to go to dinner with on weekends, drive somewhere with, or even stroll with, eating hotdogs in Central Park.

I like to introduce any man I meet and like to my other friends. Whether or not you even consider an affair with a particular man, this is a very good idea. It helps to see how well he fits in with your friends. Your friends are parts of you, almost as much parts as your arms and legs, and certainly of your mind. You and your friends feed on each other intellectually, artistically, socially, like giraffes browsing on necessary flora. A few weeks ago, when I was at a small evening party of rather intellectual and sophisticated people who often meet together, one of the group's regular shining stars brought her potentially new lover: a decent, sincere, even rich man —but one whose interests and conversation centered on hockey scores and business deals in the fur trade. It was painful to see how everyone treated this man like a curiosity, an artifact. Under these circumstances, you might decide the potential affair is worth it anyway. Or you may not (this particular woman decided against it).

I should mention that another woman who once did undertake an affair with a man she felt awkward with socially, later told us that she really didn't care that much for the man, but that she "couldn't resist because he really loved and adored me. He *worshiped* me." We sympathize with this friend's susceptibility, her overanxious desire to be loved, a need that, in the 1970s, women are beginning to call the "love myth": the myth that *to be loved* by somebody who comes riding out of the mists is all-important, rather than a view of love as a two-way thing. Two-way love is a wholly different affair from one-sided passion, as in the case of our friend's worshipful lover who was "hung up" on her in the same neurotic sense that Philip was attached to Mildred in Maugham's *Of Human Bondage*. To be swept off your feet can be dazzling, but when the romantic rush is over, the glow fades. You realize it is no great compliment to have a man ecstatic over you when he's only turning you into some sort of romantic ideal, something he sees in his mind's eye. It has too little to do with the individual *you*. The more independent you are, though, the better you can recognize this heroine-worship for what it is. And you're able to deal more wisely with it, flattering as it seems at first blush.

A sensuous feeling of well-being in an affair is something some women can create with beautiful ease. And you can, too. The more well-being the better. Your apartment is the background, the heart of the affair, and it has much to do with the source of the mood. It is remarkable how snug and comfortable one certain woman's apartment can become with a few rosy lights and a man's favorite brandy. It is remarkable, in the case of another woman, how luxurious the man in her life feels when on chilly Sunday evenings he puts on the cashmere sweater-jacket she keeps for him in her closet (and that she gave him two Christmases ago).

I know one woman who is having an affair with a man who survived four years of college on canned spaghetti and eight years of an ex-marriage on TV dinners; she was so stricken when she heard it that she became adept at making simple but delicious evening snacks and very special early Saturday evening suppers for the pair of them.

And I once met a woman who was having an affair with a man who'd had a few early years of lumberjack life in Michigan and who pined occasionally for flapjacks; so she always had the ingredients on her kitchen shelf. She mixed the batter, he flipped the pancakes. It was the kind of evening they loved. . . . As far as meals are concerned, most men say they prefer casualness to too much exquisite napery and candlelight. Occasional gourmet dinners are fine, but so is sitting on the floor and eating scrambled eggs while watching television. Not that you have to worry about it at all these days, what with men so adept as cooks that they're liable to sit you down to anything from *flambéd* little plum puddings to Maxim's version of *quiche saumon*.

This is all very cozy; but be careful: With well-being in mind, it doesn't hurt to give a man a silk robe he can keep in your apartment. And he has a great sense of luxury if he has a bathroom shelf for cologne and a set of shaving things. But you have to refrain from going overboard. Intimate as all this sounds (and is), your home is still your castle. Yours. So if you are tempted to think, for instance, *Why shouldn't he have a key to my apartment?* it is better to think again—and then to decide *No.*

I am talking about privacy again, another kind of privacy, one that's also invaluable. People can be tiring, even people you love.

Sometimes you simply want to be by yourself—no possible invasion: to be alone when you want to be, because you want the simple joy of being alone with a book or a piece of music, or of just being alone. Privacy is something you need as a renewal, a way of building the self. Any number of great philosophers have talked about that need . . . and so a few months ago did a twenty-three-year-old actress, Barbara Hershey, who said that she had a great need to *be,* and for that reason hadn't even a TV set or a radio in her house. As she put it, "My world is real. If I am lonely, I want to feel lonely. If I'm angry, I want to feel angry. I want to deal with life purely and directly." I know a woman who, for exactly that reason, goes to concerts and art galleries only if she can go alone. Only alone, she feels, can she honestly hear the music, purely and directly. Only alone can she honestly see the pictures. Living alone, you can do the same thing away from your apartment: and you can be home alone in exactly the same way. With no key but yours to your apartment door, you can *be.*

Having an affair doesn't scandalize anybody any more, at least not the way it did circa 1900 or 1930 or even 1960. Still, some social situations can embarrass you. There is, for one thing, your doorman (if you live in that kind of apartment building), and I can think of one sensitive woman who finds it agonizingly embarrassing to say "Good morning" at 9:00 A.M. to her doorman as she departs for her office, knowing that the man in her life has just ten minutes before also greeted the doorman as he departed from her apartment. There isn't any way to get around this unless you want to change your habits to suit doormen. Rather than that, it is better to keep telling yourself that doormen these days are terribly blasé.

And then, you and he, in your affair, might like to go to Europe on a vacation. Or the Caribbean. Or elsewhere. What about possible embarrassments—registering at hotels, for instance? If you're going to travel together, naïveté becomes a luxury you'll have to discard. Worldliness is more essential. When you're breaking social rules, be prepared. In Europe, they look at your passport. Some de-luxe hotels will refuse you . . . but which others will not? The de-luxe Ritz in Paris, you can find to your embarrassment, has a different attitude from first-class hotels or charming little hotels on the Left Bank. I favor the wisdom of one woman who, going to Geneva with a man who was going to lecture there on music, frankly asked her New York travel agent about the various hotels' attitudes in Geneva.

Or you might, as did another woman who was going to London, write to a friend who lives in that city, and inquire. A bright young friend of mine, once having "almost died of embarrassment" when the manager of a de-luxe hotel in Paris eyed the two passports and politely suggested two rooms, made it her business next day to sound out the tourist bureau tactfully about hotels that might be more welcoming. And I know one woman who is timid and easily embarrassed, so last year on a vacation trip in Arizona and Nevada she preferred to stop in motels rather than risk possible embarrassment at a hotel. Or you can, if in doubt, simply take two rooms—if you can afford it.

As for other social embarrassments, if you pay attention to logistics, you can usually arrange to avoid confrontations that might embarrass the grocer's delivery boy or your aunt from Chattanooga, not to mention yourself. You don't have to worry about your friends, generally. Or your business associates either. But you never know. So it is thoughtful to be reasonably discreet. In giving parties, for instance, even the most sophisticated and liberal-minded women I know give the party themselves, and Mr. X. arrives as one of the invited guests. There is also something graceful, some aesthetic pleasure in preserving a certain style, a social form.

Then there is sex.

Sex is so personal that when one begins to talk about women-in-sex, the subject is as misleading and vague as discussing women-in-general. There is no women-in-sex: There is you, the one woman you know. Cleopatra was not Juliet; Juliet was not Heloise; Heloise was not Iseult; Iseult was not Anna Karenina. But clearly all these women knew who they were, knew what they wanted, and acted accordingly. They were all real women, fictional or otherwise, in the sense that they thoroughly enjoyed themselves. A real woman is any woman who can enjoy sex and love that pleases *her* and not sex that suits popular or traditional notions. She is as impervious to them as waves pounding on a foreign shore a thousand miles away.

Where have all the lovers gone? will never be your sad plaint as long as you make love for purely direct reasons: for love, for the pleasure of an animal act, for warmth, for fun, for passion, for affection—though of course not necessarily all these at the same time. Happily, these joys are the lot of the truly independent live-aloner (or any other independent woman) who acts according to her true desires.

That kind of lovemaking has little to do with chalking up a sex score as to what you did technically well or poorly. It has nothing to do with anxiety about the sexual concepts of Dr. X., Dr. Y. and Dr. Z.—all three of whom disagree violently with each other about what you "ought" to do, think, feel. It cares not a pin for Victorian or Puritan concepts either, or whether you, as lovers, fit the sexual norm or not. Such intimidations and fears are not part of its makeup. Nor is there anything you have to "prove." That you are here together is proof enough.

Assuming that you have a reasonable amount of sex education (if you haven't, get it from good sources), there isn't much more you need to know . . . except to recognize quite pridefully that you are a unique woman among women, and he is a unique man among men, because no two people of the same sex are exactly sexually alike. So rather than being shy about talking about your particular sexual feelings with this friend and lover, you can quite pridefully be honest. This is simply allowing for the fact that lovers weren't made to be sexually compatible any more than marriages were made in heaven.

And of course if you think that your range of pleasure is possibly too limited and that maybe you could use help, it's worth taking the trouble to discuss it with a professional who understands those problems. There's certainly no reason to be underprivileged.

Quite possibly you will have an affair in which sex is secondary, as happens quite often . . . or as one well-known man who has been having a long (and famous) affair, commonly thought of as a grand passion, once said to me: "The thing between two people is not physical—if you like somebody it's mostly psychological. As for passion, if two people live together well during the day, it works well in bed—not the other way around. A man or woman doesn't really need all that much in bed."

But affairs end, too. He may end it. Or, as is much more likely *you* may: That's so whether you are older, younger, widowed, divorced. Like viruses, it is, these days, something in the air, and women have caught it, possibly for good.

Ending an affair is unavoidably awkward, though not alarmingly so. If you're the one ending it, the one thing you should be is considerate. But not everyone agrees on what considerate is. One woman who can't bear a confrontation began studiedly dropping the names of other men she pretended to find interesting; after a while the man in her life got the idea that "Maybe we should see less of each other." Another woman I know, despite a two-year-long affair, simply became less and less available: she had unbreakable dates, appointments, excuses; the hairdresser came first, or she was working on a special design project (she is a textile designer).

Complete though painful honesty is the best course. For one thing, you respect yourself for it. For another, it can transmute an affair into a friendship . . . though not often. Still, a young divorcée friend of mine who was emotionally shattered after an unsettling divorce from an erratic man, shortly afterward had an affair with an older, dependable man. He was almost twice her age, and he provided her with a much-needed feeling of emotional security. But when she regained her equilibrium, she honestly told him how she felt, and ended the affair. They are still good friends, and she is ever grateful to him.

But what if the man ends the affair?

No matter how great or undying an affair has been, it happens. Even in famous, historical love affairs, in which lovers nick their wrists and exchange blood and promises, or save each other's lives in the midst of hurricanes and earthquakes and so on, that doesn't seem to prevent one or the other from liking someone else better, later on. It is not one of the prettier aspects of life; but it is a true one. Or the men may end it for any number of other reasons.

In that case, you will hurt. But what is wrong with hurting?

Besides, the hurt eventually goes away. There are any number of ways to help it off the scene. One woman whose affairs seem based mainly on a terrific physical attraction reads books on Eastern philosophy, about how desire and the flesh don't mean that much anyway. Another woman whose affair recently ended is filling up the time with redoing her whole apartment (which really needed it). And of course if you have been keeping up your many live-alone interests, you have plenty of good things to plunge ahead with. A New York business woman tells me that the breakup of an affair always propels her into furious bursts of creative energy that result in marvelously satisfying business triumphs months later.

Surprisingly, your reaction to the end of an affair might even be relief. Some of the worst hurts occur sometimes way before an affair ends . . . or as one friend of mine once put it, "Before it ended, it was like a toothache that comes and goes away, comes and goes. . . . It was more painful *then*." The end can also be quite a relief if you've suspected that that particular affair was initially a daring and dangerous choice and could only end badly, but was nevertheless irresistible . . . or as Françoise Gilot said later of her affair with Picasso, she had sensed that it would be a catastrophe but called it "a catastrophe I didn't want to avoid."

If you're a buoyant kind of person, you might be able to get over a broken-off affair quickly . . . or you may be like another woman who is always in glum despair until the next man appears; for her, as a woman like this once told me, "It is like being hungry: If you haven't had breakfast, you're not satisfied until your next meal." Then she is all aglow again.

But whatever your personality, one bright morning to your astonishment you're likely to awaken feeling fine. Looking back on the weeks (or months) of misery, you may even ask yourself in amazement: What was *that* all about? You might even decide that the whole bittersweet intermezzo was worth it: Here you are, richer in experience, deeper in emotions, a more worldly woman, and more . . . well, more *interesting*.

CHAPTER 16

What's Around the Corner?

We've been saying, more or less, that the live-alone life in the 1970s is almost like having the right model automobile. And it gives you the cachet of being free and adventuresome, intellectually or otherwise—and the time to be free *in*.

But I have never yet encountered a situation that didn't have a root of irony. Once you've learned how to live alone enjoyably, successfully, delightfully, you're infinitely more attractive to the opposite sex. You risk getting married just when you're at last enjoying all the pleasures of living alone.

More than that, you're more likely than other women to make a success of marriage. The simple fact is that once you know how to live alone, you've learned all you need to know about *living with somebody else*. Being a whole person. In marriage or out of it. Either way, you win.

Having achieved this full hand of trumps, the wisest thing you may ever do in life is to keep in mind how valuable your cards are. Whatever old-fashioned dependency ever constricted you, imprisoned you, hobbled you, has gone the way of the tiny iron shoes worn by the early-dynasty Chinese ladies who had to be carried in litters. Now you are beautifully independent. Now you walk free. If you happen to marry, you're your own woman, able to love out of *love* (just as in an affair). You can independently pursue your own goals and let a man pursue his. *You* get a chance to be Somebody; *he* gets a chance to be Somebody. The situation is marvelously conducive to a continually exciting love, like electric sparks leaping back and forth.

You will find it easy to hang onto your independence with an unclaspable grip if you occasionally remind yourself that the independent Somebody you are is the person that attracted the man in the first place. The folly of losing that attraction should frighten you into firmly tightening your grip. If you do it right, marriage can be as intoxicating as living alone.

It might even be so intoxicating that you may never ever look back longingly and nostalgically at the joys and pleasures that graced your live-alone life.